Behaviors of Change

Timothy Christian

Copyright © 2013 Timothy Christian.

All rights reserved. No part of this book may be used or reproduced by any means, graphic, electronic, or mechanical, including photocopying, recording, taping or by any information storage retrieval system without the written permission of the publisher except in the case of brief quotations embodied in critical articles and reviews.

WestBow Press books may be ordered through booksellers or by contacting:

WestBow Press
A Division of Thomas Nelson
1663 Liberty Drive
Bloomington, IN 47403
www.westbowpress.com
1-(866) 928-1240

Because of the dynamic nature of the Internet, any web addresses or links contained in this book may have changed since publication and may no longer be valid. The views expressed in this work are solely those of the author and do not necessarily reflect the views of the publisher, and the publisher hereby disclaims any responsibility for them.

Any people depicted in stock imagery provided by Thinkstock are models, and such images are being used for illustrative purposes only.

Certain stock imagery © Thinkstock.

ISBN: 978-1-4497-8537-6 (sc)
ISBN: 978-1-4497-8538-3 (e)

Library of Congress Control Number: 2013902912

Printed in the United States of America

WestBow Press rev. date: 4/17/2013

Introduction

In 1993, the culmination of a lifelong dream to play pro football was well within Tim's reach. But then, a convergence of events changed Tim's course dramatically and his dream was squandered, resulting in depression and failure. What happened next was a miraculous, immediate transformation, a change in behavior that converted Tim's life from despair to hope. A spiritual awakening had enabled a physical transformation, a 100+ lbs weight loss, in 3 months time. But the physical transformation on the surface provided only a glimpse of the spiritual and mental transformation Tim underwent on the inside. Over the next 20 years, he validated and documented that the transformation he endured during the summer of 1993 was legitimate and permanent.

Tim's growing relationship with The Lord inspired and guided a transformational '180' 20 years ago, and this book details the strategies he developed and executed not only to change but to ensure that the behaviors of change are permanent. These strategies are presented in such a way to enable the reader to apply them to his or her life, touching on many change facets across spiritual, mental, and physical realms, establishing a credible foundation for success.

Table of Contents

Chapter 1 – A Journey ... 1
Experiences ... 2
A Need to Change ... 3
Temptation ... 4
Prepare for Change ... 5
A Journey ... 5

Chapter 2 – Doughnuts ... 8
One Night ... 8

Chapter 3 – Obesity ... 12
Growing up ... 12
My Diet ... 13
Big and Tall ... 14
Society ... 14
Obesity Rising ... 15
Judgment ... 16
Health and Your Body ... 18
Control ... 19
Why Do We Over Eat ... 19
Assess ... 21
Obesity Trending ... 21

REFLECTION – Transformation Part 1 ... 22

Chapter 4 – Who *are* You? Decision to Change Your Life ... 23
The Decision ... 23
Perception ... 24

Reflection	25
Embarrassment	28
Fuel	29
The Date	30

Chapter 5 – A Catalyst to Change   32
The Dream	33
The Real Mountain	35
Chance Encounter	36
Bible Study	38
Depression	39
Reality	41
The Catalyst for Change	42

PLANNING – Transformation Part 2   46

Chapter 6 – Develop a Plan   47
Plan	47
Discipline	48
Visualization	48
Goals	48
Contract	49
Diet	49
Exercise	49
Sustainability	49

Chapter 7 – Basic Discipline   50
Early Problems	52
Failure	52
Newly Found Discipline	54
Catalyst for Professional Athletes	55
Basic Discipline	57
The List	59
Disciplined Way of Life	60

Chapter 8 – Visualization 63
Fundamental Focus 64
Visualize Transformation 65
Perception of Others 65
Assess 66
Bridge of No Return 66
My Expectations 67
Habits and Routines 68
Eating & Exercise 68
Discipline 68
Clothes 69
Helping Others 69
An Inspiration 70
General Impact on Life 70

Chapter 9 – Goals 72
Reflection, Clarification and Planning 73
Goals Criteria 73
Example Goals 74

ACTION – Transformation Part 3 80

Chapter 10 – New Diet 81
Many Choices 82
What Can be Maintained? 83
Compounding Interest 83
Taste 83
Inexpensive 84
Dynamic 85
Simplicity 85
Diet Example 86
Experiment 87
Tale of Two Omelets 88
Working for You 89

Chapter 11 – Exercise Plan 91
Cardio Workout 92
Weight Loss Program 93
Plan to Overshoot 94
Sustained Fitness Program 95

Chapter 12 – So, What Happened? 101
Physically Speaking 101
Before Weight Loss 103
Spiritually and Mentally 110

SUSTAINABILITY – Transformation Part 4 114

Chapter 13 – You Have Lost Weight; Now What? 115
Measurement 116
The Unexpected 116
Buy New Clothes 117
Tell Your Story 117
Learn to Truly Love Who You Are (if you do not already) 118
Some May Not Recognize You 118
Work Diligently To Prevent a Relapse 118
Help Others with Action and Encouragement 118
Condition Yourself that You are a New Person to Never Return to the Old You 119
Raise Your Personal Standards and Expectations of Yourself 119
Aspire to Become a Continuous Learner of Diet and Exercise, as well as New Trends 119
Understand that You are Becoming a Legitimate Weight Loss Expert 120
Understand that You Need to Help Others with Similar Challenges You Faced 120
Develop Your Own Techniques 120

Chapter 14 – Diet and Exercise Constraints   122
Diet   122
Exercise   123

Chapter 15 – Offer and Acceptance - Your Contract   125

Chapter 16 – Behavior of Balance   129
Pursuits of Excellence can be Overwhelming   130
Consistency Not Perfection   131
Simplicity   132
Behavior of Balance   132
Behavior of Balance – Diet   134
Behavior of Balance – Exercise   134
Behavior of Balance – Weight   134
Becoming Routine   135
Not Immediate   135

Chapter 17 – Pulling Everything Together for the Long Haul   138
Little Behavioral Change Anecdotes   142

Chapter 18 – Behaviors of Change - Your Journey   144

Acknowledgements

I would like to thank the pastors, and men and women whom I have benefited from for spiritual guidance and influence.

With appreciation and gratitude to my friend Al Tierney, who provided spiritual editing, guidance, and wisdom.

I would also like to thank Bill Flint for his advice and guidance in publishing this book.

And to my wife, Sara Christian, for her advisement, editing, and love during this project.

Dedication

To my grandfathers who forged their lives in the coal mines of southwest West Virginia and my grandmothers who raised families that included my parents, Everett and Eloise; my parents who instilled values and ethics which are only surpassed by their persistent unconditional love.

And to my beautiful family, Sara, Hanna, Ellie, and Tobi, each of whom I am profoundly indebted to God.

To God, for everything.

Chapter 1 – A Journey

Is it cliché to say life is a journey? No because it is a journey; a complicated yet wonderful one. Full of laughter, tears, heartache, jubilation, highs, lows, dwelling in valleys and ascending mountain peaks, life is often directly affected or steered by wisdom, early childhood disposition, current events, and personal faith, with the latter being at the core of many. We all have these highs and lows, happiness and sadness, which culminate in our own journeys. Right now, each of us are at an important point in our own, personal journey. And most of us can say our journeys involve hope and dreams. It is likely that the depth and focus of our dreams regulate the level of stress in our lives, with fear or exhilaration sometimes entering into thoughts of the next phase of the journey. This stress sometimes causes a need for the adjustment of plans which are not always our own. The next significant shift in your journey might be in front of you. Do you feel that way? Are you in fear or are you excited; are you on the cusp of dramatic change? Is it time for you to change? Are you ready for change - for real change, inside and out, impactful and credible? Change that is lasting and credible requires behavioral and process adjustment. It requires discipline and focus, and an expectation that you must finish your life changed, inside and out, day after day, alone and not alone. Every moment.

Where are you at today in your journey, especially in terms of your health, weight, happiness, and confidence? And, what will be your mindset on your journey moving forward? Are you ready to change, willing to change, and willing to permanently change?

Are you happy with who you are, who you have become? Are you overweight? I have been there. Let's be honest, being overweight is a miserable feeling, inside and out. I bet you can list five to ten reasons why being overweight is an awful experience in your life; how you feel on the inside and outside. List them on paper. Now try to list one good reason. That's much harder to do.

Experiences

I lost over 100 lbs 20 years ago. My change process began in my heart after a spiritual awakening. The physical and mental change that followed were necessitated by the spiritual transformation. As a result, I believe at the very least, that long term change must began in one's heart.

My story, like any, has a beginning, with mine involving laziness; spiritually, mentally, and across both my diet and exercise activities. My story canvases learning the keys to simple, sustainable discipline, basic diet and exercise regimens, and applying these keys to nearly all facets of life, culminating to become the person I desired to become. My story, and this book, involve a lot of reflection on life and, throughout the book, I will ask you to reflect on your life, during which you will build a firm, carefully crafted and disciplined foundation to ensure your immediate and long term success.

I have learned countless lessons during my journey that will be explored in this book, and I am hopeful that my learnings can help you become the person you desire to become, and that eventually and more importantly, you can help other people desiring change improve their lives.

A Need to Change

It seems to begin and end with the heart. Heart disease is an epidemic. According to a 2011 report from the Center for Disease Control, "overall, 12% of adults aged 18 years and over had ever been told by a doctor or other health professional that they had heart disease". The CDC further reports that "from 1997 to 2011, the number of people aged 35 years or older with diabetes and with self-reported heart disease or stroke increased from 4.2 million to 7.6 million", an 81% increase over a 14 year period.

In 2004, my mom had her first heart attack and, in 2005, she went to heaven, losing a battle with heart disease. In 2009, my eldest brother entered into heaven far too early at 49. The cause: heart disease. Neither my mom or brother were unusually overweight nor did they consume large quantities of food but they smoked cigarettes at points in their lives, and had high cholesterol and high blood pressure. I have had grandparents, aunts, and uncles who have been diagnosed with heart disease; it runs deeply in my family. My dear mother and brother died young and as can be imagined, these events were incredibly devastating to me and my family. These events also reinforced my need to watch my health and not take good health for granted. With a beautiful wife and two gorgeous daughters it is critical to me now more than ever in my life to stay healthy, active and thin for them. Although our time on earth is predestined by our Creator, I am admittedly selfish about my health. This is one of my key reasons for staying fit: for my family. However, I was not always selfish about my health. In fact, quite the opposite; I once hated myself and health was not even on my radar.

Does heart disease permeate your family, your habits, your heritage? Are you happy with your circumstances and are you dreaming of change? If so, what are you doing, or going to do about it?

Temptation

We are all under seemingly uncontrollable pressures imposed by temptation; desires which are more times than not wrong, bad, or downright evil. Sinful temptations lie at every turn in life, literally around the corner, sometimes under the guise of 'my favorite burger joint' or 'doughnut shop'. At these locales, some of us find solace in a cheeseburger, or two, three, or maybe eight, if you are like I was some 20 years ago. Temptation. It never leaves. We must realize that temptations are never going away and we have to both tactically and strategically understand how to withstand temptation. We must understand our weaknesses and change our behaviors and strengthen our discipline to overcome the desires that drive us to dislike who we are, who we have become.

Faith has been the cornerstone driving my behavioral change. Having faith is a choice of our free will, and like choosing to lose weight and live a life renewed, it is and always has been your decision. Having faith and learning about God fortifies and strengthens behavioral adjustment, beginning in the heart. And once faith in God reaches your heart, you are afforded the power through the Lord to change your life. It begins with your free will, your choice to seek His wisdom. Losing weight and changing your life is your decision. Are you willing to change?

PROVERBS 4:23 GN
Be careful how you think; your life is shaped by your thoughts.

To properly battle and defeat obesity, you must identify your unhealthy temptations and the reasons that you want to lose weight and keep it off, and then determine how to lose weight and how to keep it off. After you have level set the important reasons that drive you to want to become a new person, execute and do it!

Prepare for Change

Prepare yourself to deeply analyze who you were, who you are, your behaviors, and who you want to become, inside and out. Credible and sustainable change must occur in both realms, one after the other, sequentially (inside then outside), to achieve real success. Spirit, mind, body. One must have an internal catalyst to drive change, and then think about who he or she wants to become, and what commitment is required before setting off on the journey and arriving at your destination. Prepare yourself to create a plan and construct a firm foundation, one with four distinct transformational phases, Reflection, Planning, Action, and Sustainability. Prepare yourself to first understand discipline and then become a disciplined person, or broaden your current discipline beliefs and practices. Then execute a realistic, long term diet and exercise program that will evolve into your new behaviors. These efforts, if strictly adhered to, will ensure success.

A Journey

My experiences, like yours, involve steps of a journey, of the spirit, the mind and the body. As you read the book, a foundation will begin to take shape, step by step across the four aforementioned transformations (Reflection, Planning, Action, and Sustainability). Each transformation is equally important to your long term success and must be completed to ensure long term, sustained change. The book is a journey into your own experiences, behaviors, and temptations, using my experiences as a basis to uncover or strengthen yours. High-level keys to the foundation are gathered in a summary and reflection exercise at the end of each chapter. Summaries culminate in finishing the foundation in the last chapter and understanding each summary requires active thought on the part of the reader, as you delve into each chapter. As you read, I hope you feel compelled to partake in reflection on your own experiences and life, each chapter requiring thinking, reacting and acting, based on your own experiences. This will provide the framework for a deep dive into your own experiences and the perceived reasons and memories that have created the person you have become.

So, grab a pen, here we go!

The Journey - Summary and Reflection

This is where and when reflection on our life begins. It is time to reflect and to begin building a foundation that will support you and your efforts to change your life. However, first, I would like to ask you a question. Are you able to reflect on your life and experiences (with respect to this chapter and subsequent chapters, where you will be asked to reflect), being very candid and honest, in order to build a foundation of lasting change? I think the answer is 'yes'. But, is your answer yes? Will you do it?

Think about your life, your journey. What has your journey been about?

Behaviors of Change

What do you want your journey to be about moving forward?

What is your expectation of your journey of change?

Chapter 2 – Doughnuts

I have a story about doughnuts I want to share. Before I lost weight, and today, my biggest dietary Achilles heel is my addiction to sugar. We all have some sort of food attractions; what is or are your Achilles heels? Salt, sugar, meat, french fries, etc? Are you able to consistently block or substitute tempting foods or do you consistently succumb to your innermost food-based urges?

I love and have always loved doughnuts! My love is not entirely about taste though. I love doughnuts because one night, my succumbing to doughnut temptation drove me to change my life.

<u>One Night</u>

The box of one dozen round glazed doughnuts was sitting on the dining room table. The simple box wielded great power over me and I felt a heavy trance fall over my ambition to lose weight. I was slowly succumbing to the power of pastry. I was in awe of the box and began to succumb. It was not that long before that evening that I had been crushed, a 23 year old devastated at how certain events in my life had transpired. But my life had since changed, along with my focus and behaviors after awakening spiritually. I had begun a new journey;

a journey of hope and change. "Enough of this", I thought.

I became frustrated looking at the box. I left the dining room and headed back to the living room to watch TV. Then I quickly jumped out of the chair and headed back to the dining room to look at the doughnuts. They looked good; really, really good. My will power and discipline were failing to evil subconscious thoughts, or the devil itself. Thoughts of "it's OK this time" or "I'll let myself slide this time" or "I give up" were permeating my mind.

It was the summer of 1993, I had moved back into my parents home after living the previous five years at Ball State University. I had spent those years at BSU as a member of the football team, gaining 60+ lbs in the process, on top of the 255 lbs I weighed entering my freshman year. I worked out hard as a collegiate football player and ate everything in sight while at BSU. Throughout those years in college, I was a regular at the local discount buffets, all night breakfast joints, Little Caesars, and, my favorite, Arby's. In fact, I am certain I was a significant player in generating Arby's profitability in the early 90's, often downing eight of their biggest sandwiches, fries and chicken fingers, with a medium diet soda, at every meal. I loved Arby's and the Arby's manager knew and loved me back. What good manager would not love me; I was an expert at turning inventories and growing profits, each at record paces. If I was not a poor college student, I could have taken Arby's to new heights, possibly even to growth areas only canvassed by McDonald's and Subway. They should have hired me as a spokesman. I was a business elevating, profiting generating, artery clogging, eating superstar. And, I was overweight.

I was a big person most of my life. During the biggest era of my life, early 1993, I had officially weighed in at

290 lbs at Scout Camp, a professional football preparatory event in Chicago, and then had ballooned up further to 312 lbs, unofficially, by June 1993. That was my peak weight. A 300-pounder. It made some sense as a football player but not, as I envisioned, a "regular-sized" person, after organized football had ended for me in 1993.

Back to my declining will power and sugar-laden trance that night in 1993. The doughnuts were fresh and primed for consumption. People with normal appetites may not have viewed the pastries as anything but tomorrow's breakfast; but not me, I was hungry. I actually love the word 'pastry', and sugar glazing over heavily fat saturated, fried dough was mouth watering. My unsuspecting parents had purchased the doughnuts earlier that day for family weekend consumption from a local grocer. They were unopened, and they were by far my favorite type of doughnut.

I was two weeks into my new life and new diet and exercise program, and had understandably been very hungry the last few days. I was charting new territory in my life with eating discipline, cardiovascular exercise, and weight loss, losing 15 lbs in the process over those two weeks; it felt great. I had already started feeling like a new man and, initially walking past the doughnuts, all I could think of was not letting myself down. Be tough; don't blow it!

I was only planning on taking one bite of "one" doughnut. I looked down at the now nearly empty box frustrated. The damage was done. I had began with nibbles and then consumed the entire box! I think I left the box itself uneaten. I had not even bothered to heat the doughnuts up in the microwave before eating them, which was how I had usually enjoyed glazed doughnuts. Was I missing any fingers? Geez. The confidence and discipline

I had built over the prior two weeks was gone and deep anger was settling in. I was mad and felt awful, nothing good resulted from my binge. But that was it; I was big my whole life and had had enough. I remember thinking I could not let that happen again. I had recently traversed depression, humiliation, desperation, and had entertained suicidal thoughts. I had left those valleys, embarking on a new exciting journey. Going back was not an option. That night, I became emotionally attached to losing weight and changing my life. This event was so important in my journey: Emotional conviction.

That was 20 years ago. I decided that night after consuming twelve large doughnuts that I would not allow myself to fail at being disciplined with my healthy journey again; at least not to that degree. I refocused my mind and my behaviors that evening, and I have not and will not ever stray again. A few months later, I had lost over 100 lbs and have since sustained my physique for the last two decades. I will never go back. I have gained an equal or greater balance of learning, focused on diet, exercise, and change. The purpose of this book is to enlighten you, underline the importance of spiritually, emotionally and intelligently investing in your efforts, and offering encouragement and help to you during your journey.

Doughnuts - Summary and Reflection

Answer this question: Are you at a crossroad in your life, in your journey, one that demands a decision which could dramatically impact the rest of your life? Are you not at a crossroad but wish you were; wish that you could change something about your life? Is it time to reward yourself with a positive, impactful change?

Chapter 3 – Obesity

In America, and other developed countries, we have more food choices at our disposal and are therefore at a greater risk to become gluttons, obese, etc. We are fat because we are human with broken human tendencies. We are fat because we lack the will to 'not' be fat. The first and most important action in changing your life is recognition of a problem you have initiated and sustained. Are you obese? If this is the case, are you culpable of your obesity? Or, do you not exercise but believe you should? Are you culpable for deciding not to exercise? Or, are you struggling in other areas of your life which were created by your own inappropriate actions; but could be corrected by appropriate actions? Are you seeing a trend?

<u>Growing up</u>

In the 70s and 80s, my least favorite activity every year, around August, was going to department stores with my mom to get new school clothes. If there was one thing I hated, it was clothes; the way they felt and the way I looked in them, if they fit me at all! I especially hated my specifically entitled clothing size – "husky". I wore husky jeans; how embarrassing is that? I was fat and did not know how to change and was so far from understanding the problem, in retrospect, it would be more appropriate to say that I was helpless. I hated my physique, was depressed, and felt that was just the way it was going to be. I was lazy, and my eating habits were deplorable. Not proudly at all, I was one of the many frontrunners in setting the ever-increasing obesity trend that would explode a few decades later.

Diet and health in the 70s were not the pronounced virtues in our society that they are today. But obesity was not as rampant nor as publicized as it as it is today either. I did not realize I was a founding member of the new obesity epidemic society of America. My parents did not know it either; no one did. I had friends and classmates who were exposed to the same foods I was but many were skinny; why was I fat? The epidemic sprouted and rose quickly across America, spurned by bad food availability, combined with competitive pricing and the lack of awareness of the dangers of obesity.

<u>My Diet</u>

I was an extreme over-eater. Although I rarely ate breakfast, I made up for the fat and calories at lunchtime – with pizza, smoked sausage, mashed potatoes and gravy, and pizza burgers to name a few. But where I engorged myself the most was the "snack" in between lunch and dinner. From the time I was about 8 years old through early high school, I enacted the same routines; after arriving home from school, before dinner was made, I would regularly slap together 3-4 baloney sandwiches with a plate full of potato chips. I can still remember the feeling of being stuffed after my daily food fests. Then, between 6pm and 7pm, I would eat dinner. More food and feeling stuffed! I seemingly could not break the habit. I was an out-of-control train, and nearly the size of one! I was overweight and disgusted with myself, and really had no clue how to change things. I was also lazy at school and my grades suffered as a result.

My parents dinner table was also full of fruits and veggies from our garden. Did I eat those? Very few times. I focused hard and heavy on the burgers, fries, fried chicken; you name it.

I am culpable. Could my parents have limited my dietary choices? Perhaps, but bad foods were everywhere and I chose to eat those foods in mass quantities; not my parents or siblings, but me.

Big and Tall

Obesity began small and grew in American homes as fast as it expanded waistlines, spurning new clothing designs and the onset of "big and tall" clothing line chains in the 1980s. I recall trying to find a big and tall retailer while at BSU in the late 80's. I did find one but had to drive to Anderson (IN), about 45 minutes from the BSU campus. There was an Arby's next to the Anderson big and tall shop. I still associate the taste of $18 worth of roast beef, chicken strips and curly fries with the Anderson big and tall store. Sad. Unfortunately, today, one can find a big and taller clothier as quickly as finding a McDonald's.

Society

How did I become overweight? It was societies fault! Not really, but sort of; maybe indirectly. Perhaps it was more socio-economic. According to "The Effect of Fast Food Restaurants on Obesity" (2009), "the prevalence of obesity and obesity related diseases has increased rapidly in the U.S. since the mid 1970s. At the same time, the number of fast food restaurants more than doubled over the same time period, while the number of other restaurants grew at a much slower pace according to the Census of

Retail Trade (Chou, Grossman, and Saffer, 2004). The study noted "the results on the impact of fast-food on obesity are consistent with a model in which access to fast-foods increases obesity by lowering food prices or by tempting consumers with self-control problems." My hometown, Kendallville, IN, was a classic American middle-class town, which, like many small towns across America, was populated by people who desire fast, low cost food choices. Along the town's main restaurant strip, US 6, there was Burger Chef (later Hardees), KFC, Dairy Queen, Redwood Drive Inn, A&W (later Pizza Hut), and McDonalds, all within a 1 mile stretch of fast food heaven. It was convenient, fast, inexpensive, and delicious.

Ultimately, my weight gain was caused simply a lack of awareness of healthy eating choices and exercise, and simple laziness. In the 70s and 80s, I only ate bad foods, and at abnormally large quantities, and I did not exercise enough to keep up; this was the essence of my behavior. As a result, I gained weight rapidly. The aforementioned study agrees, noting "Using data from the NLSY, Lakdawalla and Philipson (2002) conclude that about 40% of the increase in obesity from 1976 to 1994 is attributable to lower food prices (and increased consumption) while the remainder is due to reduced physical activity in market and home production."

<u>Obesity Rising</u>

Today, obesity figures are up and so is publicity regarding how bad obesity has become. NCSL.com reports that, from 1971-1974, 4% of children were obese. By 2003-04, the percentage had increased 4.5 times to nearly 19%. Combating obesity is made more difficult with marketing and advertising to children, luring them in through toy distribution, at leading chain restaurants, cable television food shows marketing junk foods at night and still other networks espousing to gluttony with challenging "how much can you eat" with heavily fat and calorie induced foods.

Kimberly Snyder, C.N. is the best-selling author of The Beauty Detox Solution. In a recent blog entitled "The 'Unhealthy' Food Network", Snyder blasts the Food Network claiming they are "pushing bad health." She goes on to state that "If you ever watch shows on the Food Network (and other channels that feature cooking shows), you'll find they really only judge food on three criteria: taste, presentation, and creativity. Unless you are watching a "healthy" cooking show, nutrition has nothing to do with it – and even on healthy cooking shows, nutrition takes a back seat to calories, taste, creativity, and presentation."

However, it seems that the right ingredients are being added to our societal formula to turn the problem around. With TV shows, like the Biggest Loser, Extreme Body Makeover, and diet and exercise infomercials laden across many channels for consumption, and general education on the keys to healthy living; the obesity epidemic is now highly publicized and methods to contain the problem and eradicate it are seemingly everywhere. In addition, the enlightening concept of "will power" (through control of diet and exercise) has steadily been making waves as the keys to healthy living. That said, gastric surgery is also an option for those who have treaded into morbid obesity. Obesity is a recognized epidemic that, according to the aforementioned statistics, is still increasing.

Judgment

Each year at Christmas while at Ball State, I would return home for two weeks of well-earned vacation before returning to school for the 2nd semester. Christmas vacation of 1990 was no different than any other vacation with exception to what I like to refer to as the "mall incident". I had arrived at the mall one evening, with plans to grab some pizza, do a little Christmas shopping and hang out for awhile before returning home. After parking my car, I headed across the parking lot to the mall. It was pitch black outside and the halogen lights had already turned on, scantily lighting the parking lot. About half way to the Sears entrance, I came upon a man with what appeared to be his two young sons. I was polite and smiled, but before I could say excuse me, the man grabbed his boys and gave me a look that I will never forget; fear. He proceeded with the boys to find another aisle. At the time, I had a buzz haircut and was probably 280 lbs. No tattoos or earrings. The feeling I had that night, and continue to have today was one of embarrassment and judgment. How could he judge me and not know me?

It happened again, about a year later while at a party in college. I was holding a beer in the kitchen at the party when two couples came into the kitchen. They apparently did not realize that I could see and hear them. One of the girls stared at me up and down and stated "look at how big he is; his arms, legs, etc." Now, I was working out but by no means was I a body builder. And, under normal circumstances, as a college football player, I would have been flattered; but not this time, with the tone that was expressed. The incident embarrassed me so badly that I left the party. I got into my car and drove around for awhile before calling it a night. On the drive, however, I decided once my football career was done that I was going to try to lose weight and shrink to a normal size; I was not sure how though. I planted that thought in my mind and later meditated on it during my mass weight loss. The embarrassment was seared in my mind so much that I can still remember the kitchen and the deep sense of shame and frustration.

Those emotional experiences will never leave me. You may have had an experience like that; use them to your advantage. Meditate on the experiences especially when you feel the urge or temptation to break away from your diet or exercise program. Ultimately, your desire to become thin, and resultant consistent action will be driven by your emotional experiences. In addition, judging others is unacceptable and is something you should not do.

Health and Your Body

Being overweight or obese has many adverse affects on your health. The Merck Manual states that "being obese increases the risk of many disorders". Merck goes on to say obesity increases the risk of the following:

- High cholesterol levels
- High blood pressure
- Metabolic syndrome
- Coronary artery disease
- Heart failure
- Diabetes or a high blood sugar level (insulin resistance or prediabetes)
- Cancer of the breast, uterus, ovaries, colon, prostate, kidneys, or pancreas
- Gallstones and other gallbladder disorders
- A low testosterone level, erectile dysfunction, and reduced fertility in men
- Menstrual disorders, infertility, and increased risk of miscarriage in women
- Skin abnormalities, including acne and facial hair in women
- Varicose veins

- Fatty liver, hepatitis, and cirrhosis
- Blood clots (deep vein thrombosis and pulmonary embolism)
- Asthma
- Obstructive sleep apnea
- Kidney disorders, including nephrotic syndrome
- Arthritis, gout, low back pain, and other joint disorders
- Depression and anxiety

Merck indicates that "obesity doubles or triples the risk of early death. The more severe the obesity, the higher the risk. In the United States, 300,000 deaths a year are attributed to obesity".

There is good news. "Losing as little of 5 to 10% of body weight can help lessen weight-related problems." It is up to you to reduce the risk, to change!

Control

When I was young boy, and even while in college, I did not realize how incredibly true it was that I held the keys for immediate and lasting change – change that would be applied to every aspect of my life and my core being. I would also learn, after losing weight, that the healthier I was, and felt, with a good, consistent diet and exercise, the better I feel about everything in my life. When I chose to lose weight, I was amazed at how the incorporation of subtle discipline across my lifestyle, eating and exercising, made a profound impact on my health, weight, and psyche.

Why Do We Over Eat

It is important to identify any issues or reasons that drive you to overeat. Whatever these drivers are, they must be eliminated; immediately. Separating your weight problem from any other issues affecting your psyche must first be addressed.

The American Psychological Association states that "in a society that continues to prize thinness even as Americans become heavier than ever before, almost everyone worries about their weight at least occasionally." They go on to suggest that there are three types of eating disorders:

Anorexia

People with anorexia nervosa have a distorted body image that causes them to see themselves as overweight even when they're dangerously thin. Often refusing to eat, exercising compulsively, and developing unusual habits such as refusing to eat in front of others, they lose large amounts of weight and may even starve to death.

Bulimia

Individuals with bulimia nervosa eat excessive quantities, then purge their bodies of the food and calories they fear by using laxatives, enemas, or diuretics; vomiting; or exercising. Often acting in secrecy, they feel disgusted and ashamed as they binge, yet relieved of tension and negative emotions once their stomachs are empty again. Like people with bulimia, those with binge eating disorder experience frequent episodes of out-of-control eating. The difference is that binge eaters don't purge their bodies of excess calories.

Other

Another category of eating disorders is "eating disorders not otherwise specified," in which individuals have eating-related problems but don't meet the official criteria for anorexia, bulimia or binge eating.

Assess

Some important things to assess before you begin your weight loss journey are: At what point are you starting your journey? What is your disposition in life and your state of mind? Where you start can affect everything. If A to B is weight loss, then C is the journey of sustained weight loss. Prepare yourself based on your disposition.

Obesity Trending

Obesity is an epidemic, one that has not reached its ceiling. The NCBI indicates that by 2030, "linear time trend forecasts suggest that by 2030, 51% of the population will be obese. The model estimates a much lower obesity prevalence of 42% and severe obesity prevalence of 11%. If obesity were to remain at 2010 levels, the combined savings in medical expenditures over the next 2 decades would be $549.5 billion." These are staggering increases and must be halted.

Obesity - Summary and Reflection

Are you obese? If you are, why? Bad food choices and a lack of exercise? Do you believe you are lazy? Explain.

Are you judged? Why? Are you judged because of who you are, the way you act, or the way you look? Why? Do you judge others? Why?

REFLECTION — Transformation Part 1

Who are you, where do you want to go, and who do you want to become?

Chapter 4 – Who *are* You? Decision to Change Your Life

You have had enough with your weight, your lack of self confidence, and your life. It is the time, your time, to change! There it is; done. Okay, that was easy, and as well as it should be but is that all that encompasses the decision? Emphatically, no! There is more required in developing the decision to lose weight and change your life than that. For a decision that will ultimately sustain your changed life, much more definition is required to ensure the actual decision is a lasting one.

Are you at a crossroad in your life, where an important decision is necessary? Or, have you been at the verge of arriving at a crossroad but have not had the courage to arrive? It is time to arrive at your crossroad; and it is time for you to make the most important decision you will have made in your life thus far.

<u>The Decision</u>
The very first, and most important step in losing weight and changing your life, is making the actual decision to lose weight and to change your life. Okay; why does it seem I am making a big deal out of the act

of making a "decision" to change? Well, because it is not only the first step in changing your life forever, it is also the most important step and you need to treat it as the most important decision you have ever made.

You must believe that your destiny is in the balance, because it is. You must believe that this is the most important decision in your life, because it is, next to your faith decision. When you make the decision to change your life, it should be made with deep reflection and strong serious intent and conviction. You must realize that the decision to change, and resulting action, will become larger than you; the impact on others can be dramatic.

It is important to note that proper change is thorough change, impacting all areas of your life. If you desire to change your physical presence, be prepared to change your mind and spirit; each will be impacted equally if real, lasting change is expected. In fact, with lasting change, all three areas must change. If only one area changes, long term change will be difficult to sustain. For example, if you lose weight quickly, and your mind has not been changed, you may at some point convince yourself to return to old dietary habits. If you change in your mind and then physically, but not spiritually, the risk of temptation, or guilt, may engulf your thoughts Your mind, body, and spirit must equally be strengthened and changed in effort to act in unison to defend future relapses. Either you are 100% in on this decision or you are not.

Perception

How is your personal brand; how others perceive you? I felt mine was very, very bad. I was embarrassed at certain aspects of who I was, outside and inside. How about you?

It is important that you reflect on the visible impacts

that your imagination reveals to you. You must realize that you will become a new person, inside and out, and this will impact all aspects of your life, and those lives that are part of yours. You must be prepared, in fact, that your decision may even impact many people you do not even know. Prepare yourself to become the prime living example someone else has been waiting to meet to inspire them. Prepare yourself to accept this role with confidence and gusto!

Reflection

Reflect on how you feel as an obese person, physically and mentally. Make a list and include how you feel and think about yourself and how you believe others perceive you. After you make your decision and as you are in flight on your journey, journal your thoughts and feelings about who you were and who you will become. Use the journal to inspire yourself along the journey to support your actions with a healthy dose of strength when you feel weak and are tempted to eat something bad.

Reflect on who you are with humility and accuracy. Look, we all have incredible talents and equally incredible deficiencies. Those who act as though they are perfect or have perfect lives, or who you perceive as achieved "perfection", can only be described as good actors and actresses. You must reflect with humility about where you have been, your beliefs, and about who you are today. And, this humble reflection must be accurate to appropriately set your course for who you want to become. Are you disappointed in who you have become? If so, it is time to reflect and take note on why you believe this has happened.

Now, focus on who you want to become mentally and physically. Ask yourself these questions:

1. Where are you?
2. How did you get there?
3. Where do you want to be?
4. How do you get there?
5. How do you stay there?
6. Where can you find answers to 2, 3, and 4 if you do not have them readily available?

You must reflect candidly on these questions and write the answers on paper, or computer. Keep the answers to these questions front and center. Reflect on the answers. Dive deeply into your own history. This is a very personal exercise and may become emotional or embarrassing, if you are honest with yourself. This exercise can only be fruitful if you are honest. This is an important and necessary step before you proceed further into the book. Take as much time as you need.

In my case, and as an example for you to follow, following is some of the honest reflection I experienced during the summer of 1993:

- I was overweight and way oversized.
- My diet was as poor as it could be. This was a problem because I should have been influenced at this point heavily by my experiences and training during five years of college football.
- When I played football, my physique was akin to the modern green hero that kids gravitate to. Yes, I was big and strong. But if you are thinking the Incredible Hulk you are wrong. No, my physique was more like Shrek, big, bulky, and oversized.
- I escaped college with, to my astonishment, a degree in hand. Although I had earned a bachelors degree, I spoke very poorly and struggled with

reading. I was not very astute and that needed to change.
- I had no self confidence.

These were but a few of my deficiencies identified through careful, honest and humble reflection. No one is perfect, thank goodness, but careful and honest reflection of who you are is absolutely necessary in order to understand what change is needed in your life.

Assess and examine yourself, physically and mentally. What needs to be improved? Complete a thorough evaluation of your life and how you became what you have become, and verify what specific improvement you need to make, and in what areas of your life, mind, body and spirit. This is key: Your journey must include improvement of more than diet and exercise; it must also include mental improvements like discipline and toughness or mental improvements such as intellect through reading current events and fiction or nonfiction books. And, very important, learning the proper use of grammar. In addition to losing weight, it may be time to change your hairstyle, fix your teeth, etc. My personal journey also included extensive reading and orthodontic braces. Each were significant deficiencies in my life that contributed to my lack of self confidence; I needed to make drastic improvements in both areas and so I did. I attacked those deficiencies, and I continue to be an avid learner and reader today. Incidentally, my focused areas of reading are: Bible, current events, technology and history.

I decided that I wanted to lose weight the evening before I started the journey, two weeks before the "doughnut incident". That evening, I began to visualize who I wanted to become. I had never been a normal weight, with the exception of my birth weight but I felt jubilation as my imagination wandered over the possibilities of being thin and changing my life forever. And, as I will discuss later, God was fervently at work in my heart after I let him in. I was on fire!

I thought about respect. I had never truly respected who and what I had become. I wanted that respect, desperately. I also thought about who I wanted to become. Although only you and the Lord know your thoughts, what you convey on the outside says a lot about your thoughts and who you are, your body, posture, hair, clothes, and articulation, on the inside; these are things that cannot be hidden. Understanding that reality of perception drove me hard that evening. For you, it is critical that when deciding to change, you place laser focus deeply on what you believe others will perceive in you. Maybe your ultimate goal is to create a new you that others aspire to become, but mostly because of your convictions, faith and humility. Now that is Devine, indeed.

Embarrassment

Have you ever experienced failure that has led to humiliation? Did you ignore the feelings of humiliation and moved on with your life or did you reflect deeply on it? Or, did you move on without reflection, perhaps passively, trying forget about it? Or did you skip reflection and just get angry, deflecting any causes with shallow or weak reasoning, possibly blaming someone else for the problem? I hope not.

An important aspect of permanent, lasting change is to clearly reflect on and recall the emotional, mental, and physical toll you may have absorbed after being humiliated. In reflecting, you are able to determine the root cause that spurned the humiliating event and then focus on strategies to avert such humiliation in the future.

Simply ignoring the humiliating event or getting angry without reflection on why it happened, will prevent the incredible opportunity to gain wisdom and grow from your experience.

During my decision process, I thought that if I began to lose weight, news would get around to friends and family. I thought that if I began to lose weight but then relapsed, gaining the weight back, I would feel like a failure so I focused hard on that feeling and decided that failure was not an option. I could not afford the embarrassment and would not allow it. This awareness of the impact of weight loss on not only you, but anyone who knows that you are losing weight, is powerful and can become a key in your weight loss journey. On a personal level, this awareness and perception still drives me today, 20 years later. If you can harness this awareness or expectation, you cannot fail during your journey.

Fuel

What will drive your heart to permanently change? What is your everlasting fuel? I have two sources, one being my family and the other a catalyst of change, which will be detailed in Chapter 5. This fuel can be a simple action borne of frustration felt whenever you look at the person in the mirror, based on something bad that was done to you, something you did, your belief that your level of intelligence or wisdom is low, or a common one, the way you look. You may have multiple fuel sources. You must identify your fuel, something that will keep yourself motivated today and the rest of your life. Your motivation may change; they key is to always have a source of motivation and inspiration.

It is time to detach yourself from your current obesity causing dietary practices and induce yourself with new, disciplined eating and exercise routines that become habitual. And, it is time to understand how to change your weight problem, the embarrassment, frustration, pain and hurt into fuel to drive your new self, the new gift you will soon become.

The Date

Make the decision a date to remember, reflect upon, learn from it, and celebrate it for the rest of your life. This date will become the day you effectively decided to change your life, forever. The decision you make to change your life will undoubtedly impact many people you know and do not know.

It is an enriching, powerful feeling to deeply ponder who you could become, inside and out. How incredibly exhilarating to let your mind wonder around the incredible achievements, which could later define who you will become. Drift and wonder, imagine yourself achieving an incredible goal such as losing a significant amount of weight and then imagine something more powerfully wonderful such as helping another person pull out of despair and depression, offering hope that had not been there before. You have the ability to achieve both of these and many more incredible feats.

Do not be selfish and do not hesitate. Is this the day you will celebrate as the point in time in your life when you decided to change and never return to the old life you lead? Make the decision now and celebrate.

The reasons for your decision must be compelling! One must reflect why change is necessary in their life, and then write the reasons down. Once you have written your reasons for change, that decision will be in stone.

Who *are* You? Decision to Change Your Life - Summary and Reflection

Reflect on why there is a need to change your life. Do you want to change?

Why do you want to change?

The decision to change your life is the most important decision you will ever make. Below, denote why this is the most important decision you will ever make.

Detail, in written form, why you want to change, why you decided to change and what you picture you life as becoming if you change.

Chapter 5 – A Catalyst to Change

For lasting change, one needs a catalyst to ignite your emotions to change the bad or negative behaviors of who you are, one that permeates your core feelings and beliefs, every day. This is especially true if you have spent your life being something or someone you now despise; or being overweight and unhealthy.

A basic human tendency is to relax and fall back on who and what you have journeyed into becoming in your life, because you may get discouraged, or become complacent or lazy, or all of the above. To change these behaviors, and your life, one must change all aspects of the bad to good - your spirit, mind, and body. To maintain the energy to not only change, but to sustain that change, some source of everlasting fuel to drive change must be identified and then be within your reach at all times.

It is simple to relax, and relapse; but you must not do that. To ensure relapse is shelved for good, when you feel a relapse approaching, you must be able to reach for the fuel and block the temptations. Your beliefs and feelings about who you are, and your behaviors, must all change internally in order to experience change that is lasting. What is your fuel, your internal core desire to change?

I am going to share a personal story about my life that

has become the core driver of my change success. It is critical that I share this story because it lends credibility to my journey and serves as the clear catalyst of my reasons for changing who I am. My story also has enabled me to recognize what I needed to complete a successful personal change, including a full diet and health "180", and never return to who I was. It is also important to recognize a dramatic event, or events, in your life that you may or may not have reflected on, but need to reflect on because it or they may hold tremendous value to you as a catalyst of your own personal change. You likely have an important story like mine; if you do, fully embrace it, reflect on it, and use the story to drive your change.

My personal change catalyst occurred 20 years ago; my personal relationship and experience with God. After He pounded and pounded on my door, I opened the door and let Him in. But it took a lot, including a significant, unexpected turn of events in my life, to open that door.

The Dream

I was once a weight lifter, and a very big kid. I liked to lift weights a lot but I enjoyed eating even more so. In fact, I was an over eater, an over consumer of unhealthy foods. My diet was awful and I only ran if my football coaches said we had to run. I was oversized, obese, and getting bigger. But I was also developing into a decent college football player. By my Junior year at Ball State, I had become a professional football prospect, having reached 300 lbs during my last season on the team; at the time, this was my heaviest weight. Over the course of about a year prior, my parents and high school and college coaches received letters of interest from National Football League teams and soliciting football agents. The letters from NFL teams were basically surveys attempting to gather information about my physical attributes and to measure my character outside of football. It was an exhilarating and truly unbelievable time in my life. The dream of becoming a professional football player was happening before my eyes. I felt as though I had been climbing a mountain through high school and college, aspiring to do one thing, play football, and that aspiration was coming to fruition. My heart and mind were fully engaged in my dream coming true. I had invested all of my hopes on this dream. I had received letters from over 20 agents and then chose one that seemed to be the right fit; one with several decades of experience. And my parents and I received a letter from the NLFPA (National Football League Players Association), congratulating me on my football career at that point and on my impending NFL career.

There was also another aspect of reaching the NFL pinnacle that most were unaware of. I had a chip on my shoulder the size of New York City. The chip was comprised of the memories of people who had told me I was not good enough, or told me I was failure, or those people who downright laughed at me for having a dream as big as the NFL. I had been a walk-on in college so a shot at the NFL was my redemptive opportunity; I would prove 'them' wrong. The convergence of a lifelong dream coupled with the opportunity to squash the haunting words and actions of certain people in my life who, in my mind, created the "chip", was nothing less than exhilarating. In hindsight, I never should have let the latter get to me so much, but it did.

By the time I had traversed college, after scaling some of the highest mountains in my collegiate football career, I was nearing that goal the mountaintop that was the NFL; it was truly amazing. The culmination of a dream was in front of me. But my dream would soon become a painful nightmare.

The Real Mountain

In November 1992, I played my last college football game. It was my fifth year at Ball State. I did the best I could, but through the lenses of professional football scouts, I turned in an average performance. But my performance did not deter my hope. I attended a professional football testing camp in March 1993 and performed well. The experience at the camp boosted my confidence but even with good performance my agent expressed deep concern about my chances. And something else was happening: he seemed to be losing interest in my abilities and professional potential. I had just ended a relationship with a girl, which compounded matters. My heart was sinking.

I was finishing my undergraduate education, and should have been 'on top of the world', soon to have a BS degree, but conversely all I could think of is 'this might be it'. But not 'it', meaning the end of my undergraduate education, or even football, for that matter; 'it' meant me and my life. Devastation, the horror of a football dream dashed, had firmly sat in. It is difficult to describe how concerned I was but the suicidal thoughts that permeated my mind, and especially my heart, provides a glimpse of the pain and depression I was living with. I was feeling crushed and brokenhearted. My existence was caving in around me, effectively burying me. 'I need help', I recall feeling but felt no one could help me. In addition to nearly all of my focus being on football, a friendship had abruptly ended and our family pet was terminally ill. I was becoming overwhelmed.

My only reprieve from the pain was those moments in between isolation, when some other person's presence would mask the hurting and my situation. But those quiet moments, when no one was around, were excruciating.

And then, a new, raw pain began. Through my experiences with football, I had endured a lot of physical pain in my knees, ankles, fingers, and shoulders, you name it, but I had inherited a newfound pain that I had not experienced before. A sharp physical pain had formed in my upper back that seemed to penetrate through my body to my heart. It felt like a dagger was literally stuck through me. This pain was suffocating at times and seemingly nothing could relieve it. What was it from? Then reality began to set in that my dream was not coming to fruition, and the events and people that created the "chip" in my mind were right, or perhaps all the above? I recall carrying that pain for weeks, throughout the day from the time I awoke, through classes and working out, all the way to bedtime. It was always there and I felt as though I was dying, or at least that is what I thought it felt like. I was a 22 year old kid that did not want any more of this life. How could this be happening?

> PSALM 34:18
> *The LORD is close to the brokenhearted and saves those who are crushed in spirit.*

Chance Encounter

I found myself not caring for my last semester of college, typically putting my books down to hit the gym late at night as graduation was nearing, where the weights would help me forget some of the pain. One night a few weeks before the draft, while at the student recreation gym on the campus of Ball State, I was approached by a man in what appeared to be his mid to late twenties who needed a spotter on the bench press. While spotting for him, I learned that he was a Muncie resident who was also a graduate student at Columbia in New York. I also learned that his name was John. John and I were very different. He was shorter and weighed about ½ as much as I weighed; and was substantially weaker. John was also very kind. I spotted him while he pressed 100 or so lbs and then he spotted me with over 300 lbs on the bar. We were unlikely spotting partners. We then worked a few of the machines together, hitting our shoulders and triceps. Even with his slight build, he was keeping up nicely with me. About half way through the workout, John began to talk about God. "Oh no, here we go", I thought as he asked me "do I believe in God, in Jesus"? Indecisively, I said I did not know. The ultimate cop out. John said he led a bible study at a local apartment complex off campus. He quickly engulfed the conversation in the Word. I felt a little uncomfortable. At the end of the workout, John asked if I was interested in joining his men's bible study and wrote down the apartment address, and day and time of the weekly study. My initial thought was 'no' but the address he gave me caught my eye; the apartment complex was the same complex I had lived at the year before. That is a coincidence, I remember thinking. Still with hesitation, I also gave John my number.

Growing up, I sporadically went to church. Although we did not attend church as a family, in reflection, my parents taught us using Gospel and scriptural principles: humility, love, patience, acceptance (of others). However, I did not have faith nor knowledge of the Gospel, and my spiritual focus was not on Jesus. In the late 80s, my oldest brother Al, who was a Christian, invited me to his Baptist church one Sunday. We sang and the pastor preached, focusing his sermon on the 70's hit Cats in the Cradle by Harry Chapin. I was mesmerized by connections the pastor drew between the song and our life in putting off our important things in our lives due to an ignorance of things we believe are more important. The pastor also tied the songs message with putting off our relationship with God. What an awesome sermon, very engaging. Although I never forgot about the sermon, I chose not to attend church the next Sunday and chose to put my faith off, as in the song (when am I coming home dad I don't know when but we'll get together then, dad, I know we'll have a good time then). I wish I would have continued attending church and learning; but I was stubborn.

I had thought after leaving the gym that evening that I was not up to the bible study, and believed I would not be seeing John again. A few days after working out, John called me asking when I would be attending the study. 'Boy, this guy was starting to annoy me', I recall thinking. I told him I would attend the next session, hoping if I went once, he would forget about me.

Bible Study

So, with John's invitation, the following Thursday I headed to the bible study after dinner. Driving into the parking lot of my old apartment complex was strange. I had not been to my old apartment complex since I had moved out the spring before; nearly a year had passed. It did not dawn on me until I looked for the apartment number and realized that the bible study was being held at the very same apartment I had lived at the year before! OK. This was strange given the size of Ball State, which had a student population of 20,000.

I knocked on the door and was welcomed by about 10 guys. Being overly sentimental, the first thing I did after offering a few brief "hellos", however, was gaze around the apartment and the memories from the year prior began to flood back. I think I chuckled a bit; this was more than a little strange. I began to ponder about how excited I had been just one year before. That was a depressing thought. After a few moments, I sat with the other guys and introduced myself, and shook John's hand as well, thanking him for the invitation. Although I still felt uncomfortable with the whole bible study, around the new people, who seemingly knew each other, I began to feel a sense of calm as well as curiosity as the thought of "why is this happening, the study, the apartment, etc." What a coincidence.

John began the session welcoming me and asking me to tell a little bit about myself. I was a little embarrassed not knowing anyone in the room but began by introducing myself, now to the larger group, and mentioned that I was graduating soon. I also shared with the group that I played football for Ball State and had recently been through a somewhat difficult time, with my concern focused entirely on the looming NFL draft. I continued stating that I was beginning to feel anxiety and depression at the thought of not playing football again. I felt sorry for myself. I was feeling heartbroken and let it all out; it felt good to relieve some of my pent up anxiety and fears. After I had finished, a few other guys introduced themselves to me and also said a few words. John followed with prayer, scripture readings and then a study on the chosen scripture readings.

I had a very good time that evening and felt a sense of rejuvenation but never went back to the study. A few months later, the draft would come and go, and I would graduate and leave Ball State.

Depression

Before the draft, I spent a weekend at home with my parents in Kendallville, Indiana, my hometown. The first evening back home, after dinner, my parents and I got into an argument about the future without football and I was not in the mood to talk about it. While they wanted the best for me I felt my life was ending. I had had enough. As my parents sat at the kitchen table, I was standing and noticed a knife used for dinner in the sink. I grabbed the knife and held it to my wrist, tears streaming down my face. "Stop it" seemed to utter from my lips. I was crying hard by now and was fearful. I was feeling sorry for myself, staring at my mom and dad. The fear and selfishness in my heart shifted from my heart and I felt and saw the fear leap into my parent's eyes. I knew they knew I was upset before but now I suspected they realized just how upset I was. Seeing the fear in my parents eyes broke my heart and I put the knife down. I know they loved me. I sat with them and all that I recall was a short conversation about my life being in front of me and I had so much to look forward to. They were trying desperately to encourage me. I returned to school the next day.

After returning to college, I recall sitting in my room, destroyed, crying. The pain was excruciating and I felt I was at my end. My parents had been fearful of my emotional state and had asked me to come home again or to seek help, a doctor, somebody. My mom was especially fearful, in tears herself sometimes when I spoke with her on the phone. During our last conversation she said it was time for me to pray and ask Jesus for help. I was desperate, and after hanging up with Mom, I went to my room. I began balling my eyes out and then knelt down next to my bed. Along with being desperate, I was ashamed, lost, and humiliated. With all that I had, I asked Jesus for help, praying and crying aloud.

Reality

Four of my BSU teammates were also professional football prospects. Those four were invited to pre draft pro day events conducted by NFL teams at BSU; but I was never invited. I was getting concerned. By late April 1993, the NFL draft came and went. I sat by the phone during the two-day draft event, hopeful as I had ever been; but no one called. During the days after the draft, only 3 teams showed interest for a potential NFL camp invitation but I was still hopeful. At that time, I was trying hard to conceal my concerns about what might happen if my football career was finished; I did not think that nor want to believe it. Also by April, I had gained more weight, eclipsing 300 lbs by over 10 lbs. I was eating more bad foods and consuming weight gain formula to supplement my weight gain to boot. I did not need to gain anymore weight but could not stop gaining.

Then, devastation set in as interest from the NFL began to fade. My agent signed five offensive linemen including me, in preparation of the 1993 NFL draft. The other four linemen were either drafted or were invited to NFL camps for tryouts; but I was not invited. Harsh reality was also setting in followed closely by fear. It was happening very fast, it seemed and I was afraid to except reality. I was in sinking fear that no one would want me or, at the very least, care to invite me to a camp to try out. Impossible, I thought. How was it possible that I was once sought after but now I was not even going to get a tryout? This could not be happening.

By the time graduation rolled around, I was calm. Sitting at the ceremony with my proud family in the audience, I felt at ease but not great. After graduating, I attempted to contact teams myself thinking my perseverance would lead to some type of opportunity. I should have known better. I was not letting go.

1 PETER 5:10
And the God of all grace, who called you to his eternal glory in Christ, after you have suffered a little while, will himself restore you and make you strong, firm and steadfast.

The Catalyst for Change

A few weeks after graduation, it was mid June by now, I received "the" call from my agent I had dreaded, advising me that my football career was done. After hanging up, I remember staring at the floor thinking I had to accept reality, compose myself and deliver my news to my family. I was ashamed but composure and confidence quickly swallowed the embarrassment after I turned my focus to the Lord for strength and guidance. His calm and peace showered down on me. The pain in my chest had long since evaporated and I felt hope. I did not know what exactly the hope was but I certainly felt it. That evening, I let my parents know that I had had a discussion with my agent. The news then cascaded to other friends and family.

Physical surface, bruising pain can be healed through rehabilitation, medicine and rest but emotional pain that lies deep within the unforeseen depths of one's heart can only be seen and healed by God.

JOHN 3:7
You should not be surprised at my saying, 'You must be born again.'

The day after my agent dropped the news, I made a decision to change my life, and to my surprise it felt very good. How was that possible? Giddy? Yes, and excited about the new chapter unfolding in my life. I was excited, apprehensive, scared, yet intrigued about what was about to unfold. Actually, at the time, I did not know exactly what was about to unfold in reality. Conversely, I felt I had to get away from the life I had led as quickly as possible before things went south. I knew my broken tendencies. I had a little fear inside, doubting whether or not I had the fortitude to change; I mean, "really" change. And then fear turned to raw excitement over the possibilities of what I was about to do. I recall a discussion with my mom around this time when she gave me a nugget of priceless advice, which she was good at: "you are just beginning your life and it is so important that you go after it". I did not know any better but wholly trusted her advice. That was the last ounce of fuel I needed.

I visualized all the possibilities for my life that would entail shedding a former life that was not necessarily bad but was certainly not good; at least, I was not near my potential. That included letting go of those emotions that created the "chip" in my life. And forgiving; forgiving myself and others who I felt may have wronged me. I did not have the time to be a fool and hold grudges. What would that be worth? Nothing.

I developed a burning desire to seek and reach my potential, inside and out. I felt I needed a process to achieve what I desired to do. This process, at first high level, became tactical a day to day experience that was forged through trial and error. This process and journey is captured in this book.

The journey included some very basic goals and expectations, and I immediately began new diet and exercise regimens that would later culminate in a physical transformation that provided evidence of beginning mental and spiritual transformations occurring in my mind and heart. And I felt with absolute confidence that I would be successful. The Holy Spirit was clearly with me, and 10 weeks after my decision, I had shed my former life, the pain and humiliation, and desperation, dropping about 130 lbs during that timeframe. I crossed a bridge in my life during the summer of 1993, took the intrinsic values with me, specifically my new relationship with God and my family, and burned everything else, including the bridge. I would never cross back, leaving my old self behind, for good. Amen!

We all have stories, don't we? We have complicated stories. What is your fuel or will become your fuel that will sustain you on your journey? What fuel sources will ensure your commitment to change will be permanent? In the valleys of temptations you experience, what will provide you with protection from those temptations? You need a source of strength in your journey and you cannot move forward with a sustained life change plan and action until you identify the fuel that will carry you through the forthcoming minefields of mental, dietary and physical temptation.

You may identify more than one fuel source. These could be: love and expectations of your family and loved ones, friends, or perhaps personal failures, perceived destinies, or even a simple, fundamental desire to become the person you have dreamed of becoming. Is it your personal faith that drives you? Have you taken chances during your lifetime and now realize, or have realized, that you are fortunate to have been given the opportunity to live? If so, this could be an incredible and unfathomable fuel source! It is your will and whatever you choose to provide yourself with everlasting fuel, reflect on it, nurture it, let it absorb your being and become that everlasting source of energy you need to change your life. You need to help others. There are people you have not yet met who, after you experience change, need you in their lives. As a result, you need to act now!

A Catalyst to Change - Summary and Reflection

What is your source of fuel that will sustain your change the rest of your life?

Failure can be a virtue. What have you failed at and what have you learned from failure? What was your reaction to failure, what actions did you perform to address your failings, and what were the results of those actions?

Identify, reflect on, and understand your core reasons to change for the rest of your life; your catalyst. What are your core reasons?

How is your faith in God? If you have faith in God that may be all you need for fuel. If you do not have faith, please consider it. You may be amazed at how faith can assure that change becomes permanent by virtue of complete personal foundation reconstruction on the inside (heart and mind) to the outside. For lasting change, both internal and external change must occur.

PLANNING — Transformation Part 2

Envision and plan to make change happen

Chapter 6 – Develop a Plan

"There are risks and costs to a plan of action. But they are far less than the long-range risks and costs of comfortable inaction" John F. Kennedy, 35th President of the United States of America

OK, talk is cheap. Action is what counts and you need to act now!

Let's think carefully about what has been covered thus far. You have made your decision to lose weight and keep it off, effectively creating a new you and a new life, so the next important step is to build a plan around both weight loss and sustained health phases of the journey. This critical thought process will enable you to carefully assess and develop the path you must follow to change for the rest of your life. I had a plan in mind during every facet of my journey. Having a plan will provide you with foresight and confidence of the journey you have embarked on.

Are you ready for lasting, permanent physical change? Let's discuss the high-level elements of the plan that will guide your change process.

<u>Plan</u>

A plan is necessary to assist you in creating the roadmap to where you want to go, it will keep you focused and will enable you to have a firm foundation to help when temptations are overwhelming. Temptations will arise whether they be to delay or cancel workouts, or to eat something you should not be eating, or both. The plan must be simple and of your design and limitations. The following provides the basic framework of how your plan should be constructed:

Discipline

To achieve the plan, one must understand simple, fundamental discipline and how to execute in a disciplined manner. The acts of fundamental discipline must be embedded across key elements of your life to achieve the change you expect to achieve. I will take a deeper dive into basic discipline in the next chapter, entitled "Basic Discipline".

Visualization

Before acting with basic discipline, one must visualize the weight loss journey and the journey thereafter to keep the weight off. Visualization enables you to picture what the journey might look and feel like. In addition, visualization will help you imagine the wonderful feeling that change will provide. During this process, you will naturally begin to formulate what it will take to achieve the change you desire.

Goals

One must develop simple, focused, achievable but challenging goals in order to achieve the visualized expectations of the plan. And goals will keep you on track.

Contract

One of the most difficult challenges in your journey is adherence to commitment. To assist in your commitment and to achieve your goals, one must develop a contract with oneself to ensure each goal is met. The contract will ensure you keep your commitment to change.

Diet

A necessity in achieving weight loss is the design and execution of a new diet. Education on proper dietary practices will be paramount to your success.

Exercise

To support the proper diet, one must learn what exercise program is most suitable for his/herself. Persistence in maintaining the proper exercise regimen is necessary for a successful, permanent change.

Sustainability

To achieve the plan and what was visualized, one must understand what it will take to live day to day, week to week, year to year as a new person.

This general plan covers the fundamental framework of this book. Maintaining a high level perspective of the plan, with a tactical mastery of each step in the plan, will nurture your success in becoming a new person. Today, this framework is at work in my life and I attribute it to my success.

Develop A Plan - Summary and Reflection

Develop a written plan for change that includes the basic elements of your weight loss and sustained heath that works for you. Using the elements discussed in this chapter, reflect on what your plan might look like.

Chapter 7 – Basic Discipline

PROVERBS 5:23 NIV
For lack of discipline they will die, led astray by their own great folly

After I had lost my weight, my mom told me she wished she had my will power, or discipline. She died not too long after sharing this with me. My mom raised four kids, and woke up every day at 4:30am and worked at a factory, building components in a fixed, disciplined process. Mom and Dad once had second jobs at night, cleaning offices to help the family. I sat in the offices while they cleaned. Mom even earned her GED (General Education Development) after she retired. She knew exactly what discipline was about. And, I learned everything about discipline from my parents, whether by Mom's day-to-day regimen or by seeing my dad awaken at 3am to work at a foundry over several decades. They are my heroes.

In America, action and the results of disciplined behavior are happening all around us. At home, school, work, in toys and gadgets, travel, stores, discipline is a common ingredient of our lives. We know what it looks like, but do we execute in every aspect of our life with discipline? Likely not. And often, when we are exposed to disciplined behaviors and requirements at work, where our living is made, we conversely allow undisciplined behavior elsewhere; such as with our health. If this is true in your life, it must change now if change is what you desire.

Establishing a behavior of discipline is a requirement in your weight loss plan and long term weight loss. What is discipline really? The Merriam-Webster.com dictionary describes discipline in several ways, but the one most pertinent to the subject at hand follows: "a rule or system of rules governing conduct or activity". This definition best describes the type of discipline one needs to lose weight and then keep it off.

Outwardly disciplined people are impressive. Marathoners, professional athletes, service men and women, academic geniuses, etc. The discipline that people who fall into these categories is advanced. Marathoners may run many miles per week in effort to properly train for races, professional athletes work tireless hours outside of what we see when they perform in competition, and service men and women risk their lives regularly to ensure that Americans keep our freedoms.

Some people believe obese people are lazy and incapable of being thin. That is a worthless claim but maybe it is true for a few obese people but not for all. There could be a hereditary problem, a physical ailment or it could be a combination of one of the aforementioned with misplaced or undiscovered discipline. Misplaced or undiscovered discipline - what? What I mean is you may be overweight and lack the needed discipline with diet and exercise, but you are very likely already exhibiting discipline in many other parts of your life, such as work, school, friendship or family loyalty, trust, integrity, etc. Discipline is not an art nor is it science. Discipline just 'is'. And whether success is linked to people, companies, institutions, or sports teams, discipline is a common staple among all four.

Early Problems

I have a couple of examples of undiscovered discipline and persistence that I learned and applied early in life. One learning resulted from academic problems.

In elementary school, I nearly failed 4th grade after failing math but averted that reality after being given a chance at redemption through several weeks of summer school. Then, in 7th grade, I failed reading. Fortunately, help came through remedial reading courses that were conducted while my classmates completed the standard course material during class. But the whole exercise came with humiliation. Every week, I would leave my class and meet with a teacher's aid to cover the basics of reading while my classmates watched me leave the classroom. Those failures became successes through help given to me when I needed it desperately. Luckily, in both instances, I also learned a valuable lesson about discipline that I have carried in my heart since. My failure a decade later during my pursuits to play football professionally were not supplemented with any help.

Failure

Adversity has the effect of eliciting talents which, in prosperous circumstances, would have lain dormant. -- Horace

The second example of undiscovered discipline and persistence that I learned and applied early in life occurred in high school. This learning resulted from athletic performance problems.

Have you ever failed at anything publicly, in an

embarrassing way? I would imagine many of you have and it's not a bad thing, at all. And public failure at a young, impressionable age is seemingly disappearing. The following statement from an April 12, 2012 article by Michael Sigman who writes for the Huffington Post captures the problem well. "America's 'everyone gets a trophy' syndrome has become a national joke. 'A' grades, which once conveyed excellence, are now given to 43 percent of all college students, according to a study by grade-inflation gurus Stuart Rojstaczer and Christopher Healy'. It is a dangerous joke. Whenever your are not challenged, or do not take a challenge seriously, it is all but impossible to improve your disposition, be it a lack of intelligence, strength, or both. In any regard, weakness and failure will persist.

I have had a few public failures, one being a presidential fitness test in 1984. I missed on all tests, in front of my classmates, failing miserably on pull-ups (where I squeezed an impressive "0" pull-ups) and then I followed that performance up by completing an awe-inspiring 9 pushups; on top of that, I was overweight. It was our first couple of months in high school, a consolidated school that pulled together eighth graders from 3 separate schools. It embarrassed me enough to isolate myself from the new friends I had recently made. Rather than sulk, however, I decided immediately that I had to change my habits; at least the exercise portion. I used my public embarrassment to fuel my new self, driving me to exercise for the first time in my life. It was clear to me later, when in college, that pull-ups and push-ups embarrassment experience was the defining "exercise" moment in my life. After 30 years, I am completely convinced. As powerfully embarrassing as it may have been, it very possibly was one of the richest, most influential learning experiences I ever experienced.

That morning, the "embarrassment event", I had driven some of my classmates to laughter by pushing 9 pushups, barely, far below the expected number of the presidential fitness test. I had then spent the rest of the day at school embarrassed for myself, frustrated, and mad. So that evening, I learned something about myself that I had, until that time, kept closed away. I learned what channeling was: channeling frustration and anger into something positive. I also learned that change can be simple or complex, depending on how it is approached.

<u>Newly Found Discipline</u>

That night, I began doing pushups; with frustration, anger, and passion. I kept it simple; I had to increase my push-ups now because I could be asked again at the next gym class to perform again. This decision, keeping it simple, was the key, a founding principle I lived by in college and since I have been a professional. Why over-complicate when you can miss the key, simplistic point(s) that will really drive your success? I focused on pushups because my performance in that exercise test earlier that day embarrassed me the most. I knew I could do 9 pushups, based on my test results earlier, so I decided to focus on something less than 9 and do sets. I began with 4 sets of 5 pushups, giving myself a 60 second break between each set. I did this every evening that week, and continued for the next two years, seven days a week. Within a few weeks, I was up to sets of 10 pushups! Within a few months, I could push out sets of 20! An unbelievable transformation! My confidence exploded.

I used those simple lessons in discipline to fuel my focus and performance to drive success in high school and college athletics. Ten years later, I used the same principles to lose weight rapidly. And today, 27 years later, I still do pushups (sets of 40), using the same simple techniques. Simplicity and discipline are keys to success. How many pushups can you do? And, how quickly can you double today's number?

Catalyst for Professional Athletes

When watching athletes perform at the professional level, it's easy to appreciate their physical talents, expressing their gifts doing amazing things. What many of us do not see, however, is what many athletes must do to achieve their sometimes record-breaking feats. Many are as gifted with discipline as they are with whatever sport they are competing in. Some of these athletes, in fact, probably would not be who they have become without basic, sustained discipline. Following are a few stories of my favorite all time, disciplined athletes who have made it to the top of their respective crafts:

Albert Puhols

"He practices. Diligently, with serious discipline. Every day, no matter what. When he's tired, he still practices. When he doesn't feel like it, he practices. When he's going great, he practices. When he's in a slump, he practices. Get the picture?"

Michael Jordan

Melissa Issacson wrote that "There was a perception of Michael Jordan that he could never survive retirement because there wouldn't be 20,000 fans cheering him at the golf course or gas pump. But if you believed that, then you never saw him at practice, where all that mattered was the kill."

Larry Bird

In "Habits", Darren Hardy notes that "My dad used Larry Bird as an example to teach me about habits when I was a kid. "Larry Legend" is known as one of the greatest professional basketball players, but he wasn't known for being the most athletically talented player. Nobody would have described Larry as "graceful" on the basketball court. Yet, despite his limited natural athletic ability, he led the Boston Celtics to three world championships and remains one of the best players of all time. How did he do it?

It was Larry's habits—his relentless dedication to practice and to improve his game. Bird was one of the most consistent free-throw shooters in the history of the NBA. Growing up, his habit was to practice five hundred free-throw shots every morning before school. With that kind of discipline, Larry made the most of his God-given talents and kicked the butts of some of the most "gifted" players on the court."

Walter Payton

Joseph Staph wrote in "Walter Payton's off-season training" that "Payton's off-season training routine was so challenging that it became legendary among other professional players. In addition to lifting, Sweetness pushed his already-fatigued body with daily gut-checks in the Mississippi heat. He found a sandbank by the Pearl River, near his hometown of Columbia, and laid out a 65-yard course, which, by his own estimate, equated to 120 yards on hard ground. He ran countless sprints through the course and back, because he believed that the sand made his legs stronger and allowed him to cut better at full speed. To make things even tougher, Payton purposely ran during the hottest hours of the day. The air was warm and thick, and the sand was so hot that he couldn't stand still between sprints without blistering his feet.

Describing those workouts, Payton once said, 'You get to a point where you have to keep pushing yourself. You stop, throw up and push yourself again. There's no one else around to feel sorry for you.'"

Two of the most incredible people I have ever met are Donnie Ray Crozier and Allen Christian. Donnie is a pianist and is my wife's uncle. What is amazing about Donnie, now in his 50's, is that he has been blind since he was four after a rare disease caused his blindness in both eyes. However, Donnie overcame his disability and self taught himself piano after becoming blind. He has made a career as a pianist and singer.

One of my earliest memories of Allen Christian, my brother, was his persistent practice with music, seemingly every night while I was growing up. He worked tirelessly at his craft, and had a second job playing in bands at local establishments. He worked so hard to perfect his talent, and it left an impression on me that I will not soon forget. One of the common themes in his love of music was discipline.

These are stories of discipline. You must understand, enact, and perfect basic discipline to provide the foundation for lasting change.

Seek freedom and become captive of your desires; seek discipline and find your liberty. -- Frank Herbert

<u>Basic Discipline</u>

To lose weight, you can create a plan that includes advanced discipline such as described above. But is that type or level of discipline needed to lose weight and keep it off? Absolutely not! In fact, a basic and intermediate discipline is likely best suited for weight loss and sustained weight loss, respectively.

Behaviors of basic discipline include

List
- Develop a check off list that includes, at a high level, all tasks you intend to complete today. This list might include mowing the lawn, groceries, workout, work, pay bills, etc.

Execute to the list
- Develop a new list tomorrow

Workout
- Complete a workout for 30-45 minutes, 4-5 times per week

Diet
- Ensure the diet includes a balance of fruit and vegetables

Now, taking an aspect of your high level checklist, such as your workout, add specificity. For example: within the aforementioned workout time constraints, 30 minutes will involve cardiovascular exercise and 15 minutes will involve weight lifting. The key is discipline. Note that a workout regimen will be explored in a later chapter.

One must recognize, respect, and enjoy discipline and character, and plan to lead a new life with these founding principles affixed to who you are, before you can change yourself, inside and out, and change the person you are the rest of your life, and beyond.

Before losing weight, one must grasp the concept of

fundamental discipline. In losing weight and keeping the weight off the rest of your life, one must master the fundamentals of discipline. Building your life around discipline will enable success in your journey. Notice I did not say becoming a master of discipline but a master of the fundamentals. Big difference.

Becoming a master means your every thought and effort involve succinct planning and execution. Being a master means you do not accept failure and you consistently push yourself to your mental and physical limits. Picture a professional marathoner.

Conversely, mastering the fundamentals means you understand what discipline is; you have developed a basic discipline plan and executed it consistently, and you have achieved something important to you as a result. Additionally, you develop habits and routines around basic discipline principles and you lead the rest of your life in this manner.

Now picture developing a list for groceries, cutting coupons, setting a goal for spending, and then executing to that goal. Very simple and very doable. Mastering the fundamentals of weight loss and sustained health can be as simple as achieving the grocery spend. The difference with weight loss is that you must understand the fundamentals of physical exercise and master the fundamentals of discipline around physical exercise.

The List

The list is critical to discipline. A list can be as simple as a pad of paper somewhere where you can get to it easily, with ease, being of key importance. I recommend that you develop your own list, one that you can be proud of, one that caters to you and will help you achieve your weight loss plan. I have used both paper and electronic lists over the years and I have learned that (1) there is no perfect list, (2) the list process must be easy and repeatable, and (3) the list and process must be of your design.

The list, whatever style you design or use, will become a method for you to see the change that you are creating, day by day. Specifically, like most of us, you likely see yourself in the mirror on a daily basis. During the course of weight loss, you may not notice a great deal of change during the process. Although others, who have not seen you in a while, will see change, sometimes dramatic, you may not. The list, or checklist, will provide you with reinforcement that, yes, change is occurring by my daily investments.

This list, in itself, will become a confirming, sealing act to you that you have arrived as a disciplined person. The list, if you use it like I do, will become your daily companion (even on the weekends), fortifying your quest to lose weight and keep it off. Psychologically, my daily lists regularly ignite my drive and fulfillment.

Disciplined Way of Life

Discipline can be basic, intermediate, or advanced. People may be classified as within one of these areas of discipline. To achieve sustained weight loss, you must experience and travel through these areas of discipline. Advanced to intermediate for initial weight loss and dieting, and basic for sustained weight loss and diet.

Discipline begins and ends with humility. How receptive are you to criticism and what do you do with accurate criticism when you receive it? Do you ignore the accurate criticism and become hurt, hardened in heart, or frustrated, or do you let it go through one ear and out the other? Or do you reflect on it and desire to understand why you were criticized; and work to get better? How

Behaviors of Change

do you operate with respect to criticism? If you are one who accepts it, reflects upon it, and humbly looks in the mirror to validate it, and then changes as a result, you are a person of character. Understanding this is critical to your weight loss journey.

As discipline becomes a greater focus and driver of how you live your life, so does your character. The resultant effect is change. And, an important thing to remember is your capacity to be disciplined and to exude strong moral character in your heart, thoughts, and actions is great.

If you understand the criteria of discipline, if you recognize good, accurate criticism and understand that you are to become a better person if you apply yourself, you are well on your way to achieving the change in your life that you desire.

Discipline - Summary

- Develop a coachable, receptive attitude, receptive to criticism.
- Discipline is required for lasting, credible attitude change.
- Basic discipline is the key. Do not become a master of discipline but master the fundamentals of discipline.
- Start light, small. Build an effort and understanding of sustenance through the process. This way, when you are at a level which can be sustained the rest of your life, it will be natural to you. Starting too fast, too strong, will lead to short term gain, long term failure.
- Develop your own behavior of discipline.

Discipline - Reflection

Are you a disciplined person? List routines you follow daily, weekly. Now list in what ways you can be more disciplined, be it physically, mentally, or spiritually.

How can existing or newfound discipline behaviors be utilized during your plan to change?

Do you develop daily tasks that keep you on track? If not, why not? Is it time for you to make lists that hold you accountable to your expectations?

Develop a list of activities for today and execute that list.

Chapter 8 – Visualization

Preparing yourself for change, before you begin to change, is as important as the act of executing change during the journey; you prepare by visualizing. You must visualize and condition your mind for the impending journey that will change your life. Before you begin the physical process of change, deeply visualize what the process might look and feel like to you. As discussed previously, recognize that change needs to occur in the mind, body and spirit to be lasting. Recognize that change will be difficult and prepare to be challenged. Be excited that every effort you are about to make is an investment in changing your life. You have just won the lottery, your decision to change, and now it is time to enjoy the fruits of winning. What are the affects of change throughout every aspect of your life?

Actions alone are an important factor in your weight loss journey and sustained health, but health must be accompanied by other elements to ensure your action is not made in vain. It begins with thoughts of "what will my life be like"?

During your change journey, you must be receptive to change, to be coached and developed. You must prepare your spirit, mind, and body for change, and expect change to occur in all three areas of your life. What is your capacity for changing these areas of your life? If you have a low tolerance to change, this is an area of your life that you must confront and improve, dramatically. You need to be willing to change, and change permanently, to succeed! If you have any tolerance to change, any unwillingness, you will fail at some point in the journey. You must have and live with humility, fully, in order to recognize the depth of change you need to undertake. Look at yourself in the mirror and confirm your readiness. If you are not ready, not humble, at some point your lazy ego will take over, consume your being, preventing the rigors of change from taking shape. Be humble about your faults, and respectful of other's faults as well.

<u>Fundamental Focus</u>

The evening I made the decision, I focused on what I should do to begin the journey. In 1993, when I lost the weight, there were few easy-to-find weight loss diet options and even fewer tasty diet foods. And the internet, as it exists today, had not been invented. Instead of researching at the library or local bookstore, I once again focused my mind on fundamentals: food, consumption and quality, and exercise. What could I do, fundamentally, to begin the process? Well, at the time, I was eating as poorly as one could and, although I was working out, I was only pushing weights. So, to begin the process, and what I would later learn were the keys to diet and long term weight maintenance, I focused on the basics: lowering fats and calories in my diet and introducing, slowly, cardiovascular exercise into my workouts. That fundamental focus was and is paramount to weight loss and long term weight loss maintenance. Period.

I would also later learn that keeping a perfect daily

diet and exercise program was not as important as understanding the big picture: how is my weekly and monthly diet? See, you burn calories all the time breathing, while you are awake and when you are sleeping. As a result, diet and exercise is more like cash flow; you are constantly calorically crediting and debiting your body. Your day-to-day diet and exercise should not be your focus – but your basic diet and exercise, generally, should be your focus. Do not worry yourself over periodic lapses but focus on the big program. If you can focus on the overall program, the "big picture", and allow periodic diet and exercise lapses, you will not fail. Now, periodic lapses should not occur daily but maybe once a week or every few days (at most). Understanding the difference between a good diet/exercise program and what a lapse look like is essential. This will be discussed later.

Visualize Transformation

While you are transforming yourself, your day by day journey can become overwhelmingly boring, if not suffocating. The transformational journey can feel like a long road trip, driving from small town to small town, with corn fields in between; same town, same corn and you feel like you are getting nowhere. Same routine, every day, at the dinner table and at the gym. Boring! How can you make the process exciting?

Perception of Others

What will your family, friends and acquaintances think of the new you? Will you have a positive response? What if the response is negative? Both outcomes are possible, and likely.

Assess

The first thing I did after deciding to lose weight was assess my diet and exercise. It was simple; I wasn't doing anything right before I began the new weight loss diet, with respect to losing weight. I was eating everything, sparing nothing but the tire forming around my waistline, and I was working out with heavy weights. Basically, my formula produced bad weight, just the opposite of what I wanted to accomplish. Can it be that simple? Yes.

Losing weight is part of the challenge; keeping it off is a completely separate challenge unto its own.

Before beginning my weight loss, my life changing venture, I reflected on my life, and the things that led me to where I was, and dreamed of my new life. For as long as I could remember, I had always been overweight but desired to be like people who, because of heredity or their own volition, were fit. Do you feel that way? Admiration turned to frustration when some of the fit people were not trying to be fit, but were naturally in good shape. I channeled the admiration and frustration together to fuel my passion for fitness and for becoming skinny. I was fed up with the humiliation. I wrapped my mind around my expectations and around everyone's perceptions of me. That reflection and day dreaming fortified my determination to become thin. I decided to focus on admiration, frustration, humiliation, and channeling for more fuel to drive my passion to change.

Bridge of No Return

After you lose weight, you will have crossed a bridge, at least figuratively. In becoming a new person, thereby crossing the bridge to the new you, one must never cross back to the other side. After you cross the bridge, turn around and dismantle it so that you never cross back over it. Dismantle the bridge by reflecting on who you were when you began your first steps across the bridge, and the hurtful feelings you had just being who you were. Seer those thoughts on your heart, ingesting the pain you felt and make a pact never ever to feel that way again. Grasp the things you deem important to take with you to the other side, and then burn that bridge down, rip it apart and throw it down the ravine and watch (and feel) the bridge pieces float away forever. Stand on the other side reveling what you accomplished. Chapter 5 explored this concept.

My Expectations

It is critical to accept a stance and then follow through with on changing your bad habits immediately. Prior to change, I, like you, needed to make a relentless assault on all of my bad habits until the bad behaviors, which had caused me to fall into the state I was in, were changed. What will this look and feel like in your life, specifically?

My early thoughts prior to weight loss were consistent with how I feel today. What can I do to sustain a healthy lifestyle once I lose the weight? Building a foundation in any endeavor is the most important task to accomplish. Losing weight is no different. Back in the early 90s, fat free and low fat foods were rare, and if they existed, they lacked flavor. I set a precedent in my mind that my eating habits had to change, even if taste was nearly nonexistent.

What would others think? In my mind, I pictured everyone I knew either saying "you can't do it" or "we are so proud of you for doing it". I tied emotion early to success; this was key. Later, during my weight loss workouts, I would focus on my emotional tie to my weight loss goal to sustain me through the end of the workout.

Habits and Routines

What kind of habits must I adapt to ensure my investment in weight loss lasts for the long haul? This is as an important question as any other. The habits you develop, nurture, and live by will provide the framework for success. So I first focused on developing good habits, specifically discipline, good early habits, and good exercising habits. Begin to understand what good habits look and feel like.

With developing habits come new routines. I thought 'what type of routines must I act out regularly to sustain any weight loss'? For me, I knew I would need new eating and food choice habits and routines because of my natural tendencies were to overeat bad foods. In hindsight, good habits and routines, from dawn to dusk, provide the framework of success. Since losing weight, I have kept my core routines around diet and exercise; these will be a part of who I am the rest of my life.

Eating & Exercise

I reflected on how my eating and exercise program will never be the same. This was a suffocating thought at the time but I knew it was a requirement for success.

Discipline

As discussed in the previous chapter, you must develop a behavior of discipline. Discipline, required to execute and sustain good habits and routines, would inevitably become facets of my entire life. While a collegiate football player, I always looked forward to post season, when I could finally relax and be a normal student. Relaxing to me was not working out as much and not running at all. For me, post season was akin to winning the lottery! I could relax, put my feet up, maybe open a book to study and just vegetate. Back then, I had an awful diet so that would not change in post season. Post weight loss, I envisioned not having a "post season" but instead a continual season where discipline was a way of life. I focused on committing to this, feeling this would become one of my biggest challenges.

Clothes

I reflected on what new clothes I would need to buy. Before that, I thought how will it feel to not be constrained in clothes? I had know idea what to expect! My entire life, I always had dreaded clothes shopping, from early memories of school shopping with my mom to trying to find low priced big/tall shops in my early twenties. I was going to experience a change in what clothes meant to me and literally, physically felt like to me, and that was an exhilarating, freeing feeling. How about this thought? How do I want to feel and look?

Helping Others

Something I began to ponder during my weight loss journey was helping other people. I was getting compliments left and right and I felt overly compelled to help others in need to do the same. For me, in hindsight, this has everything to do with my faith and humility. When you lose your weight, and sustain that weight loss, you will have exposed a talent, an ability that you have always had. It is there. During the process of exposing the talent, others will admire you, some of which are desperate to know your secrets. Within you is their key to success and happiness. If you are driven to lose weight, and you are successful at it, do not take for granted the gift you have received. Share it and your fruit will return in countless ways, spiritually, mentally, and physically.

Spiritually, you will please God; there is nothing better than that. Mentally, it will energize you to keep going and sustain your success. Physically, well, that is taken care of by the first two.

An Inspiration

I found during my weight loss journey that I was becoming an inspiration to others. This is a gift from God. Once becoming an inspiration to one person, I reflected on this, humbly, becoming a way of life for me. Simply reflecting on being an inspiration to someone lights an inextinguishable fire inside you.

General Impact on Life

I reflected on how my attitude and personality might be impacted by weight loss. Honestly, looking back, I had no idea what has happened would happen. Frankly, I am not the same person I was before I lost weight in 1993. I know my loved ones who knew me before and know me now would attest this fact. For me, it began and will end with my spirituality; everything else cascades from that.

Take the time to deeply reflect on the process to lose weight and the journey to becoming a new person. Enjoy what could be and then enjoy the ride.

Visualization - Summary and Reflection

- Think about what it will take to lose weight.
- Visualize your transformation.
- Reflect on how you will be perceived differently than today. How does that make you feel?

Behaviors of Change

Prepare yourself for change by reflecting on what life may be like after weight loss has occurred. Explain, in detail, what life you foresee for yourself.

Habits and routines are required to drive sustained success. How will these impact your life day-to-day? How will routines impact your success?

Chapter 9 – Goals

In chapter 6, we discussed a fundamental plan to lose weight and then keep the weight off, while in chapter 8 we reviewed the process of visualizing the act of weight loss. Executing the plan and experiencing the desired weight loss requires specific, measurable, and achievable goals. However, establishing and following appropriate goals for weight loss must be a consistent practice or your intentions and efforts might be wasted. This reality could lead to short term and long term failure.

I find it fascinating that many people sometimes plan their vacation and grocery lists with more clarity and better care than they do their general health and well being. Perhaps that is because escape and or pleasure is easier than change. Or, this fact is based on need, the need to eat, find foods fast while at a store, and to ensure the bank is not broken in the process. The planning part of losing weight and changing your life requires reflection and observation, slowing down to clarify the rights and wrongs of your failing diet and exercise habits. The effort to lose weight will also require focus and detail planning, and the same execution if you are serious about achieving results. Action effort requires appropriate planning and goals.

Reflection, Clarification and Planning

Before I began my weight loss, and during the early stages of weight loss, I focused all thought on changing my life and it felt exhilarating. As discussed in an earlier chapter, I really felt like I won some type of lottery (or that was my perception because I have never won the lottery). Or maybe the feeling was more akin to leaving prison? Either way, it was exhilarating. The process to lose weight clearly began with reflection and deciding what I wanted to do (chapter 4). Action to achieve the plan is the next step but setting the specific and achievable goals to support your planned action is the bridge between thought and action. The goals you create to guide your effort, if appropriate, and if followed, will enable your success. I had two general, high level goals when I began: Lose 100 lbs and fix my crooked teeth. Although these were the two main focuses, sub goals were created and cascaded from the two high level goals. I also felt that I wanted my change to be more transformational. So I decided that I wanted to improve my command of grammar. So I added reading to my top two goals of weight loss and braces.

Goals Criteria

So, the key high level goals I set were: (1) lose 100 lbs, (2) fix my teeth, (3) and improve my knowledge and command of grammar. But now more clarity and specificity must be incorporated; other criteria must also be considered.

The following criteria should be considered when developing goals:

- Goals provide you with a target, enable focus on specific expectations, and also bring joy in achieving them.

- The goals must be fundamental, specific, and must adhere to numerical elements, in this case weight loss, caloric intake and/or time.
- Goals must also address any knowledge deficiencies you have about aspects of your journey, such as what is a healthy diet for you? There are likely options. What foods or vitamins should I supplement my diet with during the journey? If you do not know these then one goal might include educating yourself on supplements and vitamins.
- Another aspect of knowledge expansion may include understanding energy loss; how do I ingest energy properly and maintain optimum energy levels, without ingesting too many calories.
- Specific timing requirements must be set.
- Identify any circumstances that may hinder you from reaching your goals. Develop mitigation plans to address those.
- Chart your progress and celebrate achievements.

<u>Example Goals</u>

Once you have commandeered what goals you intend to follow, based primarily on your weaknesses that as of today are long hanging fruit, and understand the fundamentals of goal development, it is time to put pen to paper. Following were my goals from the first year of my change:

<u>Purpose</u>

Lose weight (100 lbs), have my crooked teeth corrected, and improve grammar.

I felt this purpose, if achieved, could be well-rounded and life-changing for me. Your purpose has to be as demonstrative and achievable. In addition, to weight loss, what are your game-changing goals?

<u>Specific Goals</u>
Now, take the aforementioned high-level goals and develop specific goals that support them (that is your high-level goal).

<u>Mental</u>
Assuming your change program is starting in June:

- Learn basics about nutrition and proper dieting. Select book by July 1 and finish by August 31.
- Learn basics about cardiovascular exercise by July 15.
- Obtain and listen to a grammar improvement tape collection.
- Review your diet and exercise plans with your Dr. for input.

<u>Physical</u>

- Establish a regular workout philosophy and execute. That is, I will run on a treadmill, outside, or equivalent cardiovascular exercise, 5 days per week before 6am. If I miss one of my 6 am workouts, I will make up that workout the same day before 1pm.
- I will rest no more than 1 day per week and not workout.
- Maintain energy by eating low fat or fat free snacks regularly.
- Stair machine at least once daily, 7- days per week.

- Sauna once daily
- Weight training at low weights and high reps 2 days per week.

An exercise plan is discussed in detail in chapter 11.

<u>Diet</u>

- I will establish my regular dietary foods.
- I will establish the frequency I will allow myself to cheat.
- Remove all fat laden foods from my diet immediately with no cheating whatsoever until I arrive at a weight I feel comfortable at.
- Ingest only low fat or fat free foods.
- Do not ingest any foods after 6pm.

Dietary specifics are contained within chapter 10.

<u>Weight Loss</u>

- 25 lbs in first 6 months
- 50 lbs in first year

<u>Risks & Risk Mitigation Plans</u>

- I have children, spouse, or partner who may prevent me from following my goals. See constraints later, in chapter 14.

What will your initial goals look like? I would recommend that you stick to specific, fundamental goals initially. If you need to, please copy mine.

The aforementioned example goals are for guidance

only. Develop your own goals that fit your development needs and lifestyle. Ensure your goals are specific and address your fundamental deficiencies. Ensure that your goals are difficult to attain yet are attainable; this is at your discretion. Even if your goals are simple and easy to achieve, achieving them will provide reason to celebrate.

Plan to review your goals and chart progress along the way to validate your efforts and to provide you with reasons for the efforts required along your journey. And, after you create new goals, reflect on your accomplishments; revel in how far you have climbed. But then, move on to your next challenge.

Goals are important for weight loss but not for weight loss sustainability. Weight loss is a project with a beginning and an ending, whereas weight loss sustainability is more of a lifestyle commitment, with no ending. In chapter 13, we will discuss transferring your goals to a contact.

Goals - Summary and Reflection

- Specific, achievable goals are required in order to reach your sustained weight loss plan; in effect, you new life.
- Develop simple goals but they must be specific to address the appropriate areas of change.
- Review your goals and chart your progress. Celebrate and move on.
- Focus on the first part of your journey. Are new goals needed to continue? If so, what are the facets and expectations of your new goals?

Hebrews 12:11
"No discipline seems pleasant at the time, but painful.

Later on, however, it produces a harvest of righteousness and peace for those who have been trained by it."

<u>You Just Did It!</u>
Based on the act of making the decision to change by the lose weight and become healthy, reflecting on the reasons for that decision, enacting faith in the process, developing goals to address the decision, and by signing a contract, guess what? You are a disciplined person. Executing your program based on your efforts you have invested to date is next. In executing your program, you will now begin seeing the fruits of your desires, planning and efforts.

You are now experiencing behavioral changes with respect to how you view yourself, discipline, exercise and food. With respect to food, I decided to convert my feelings of enjoyment in eating very tasty, bad foods until stuffed; to enjoyment about eating tasty healthy foods. This was a vital behavioral change proving pivotal to my success; and still holds true today. This type of conversion must take place in your life as well to ensure your success. That does not mean removing the occasional enjoyment of the sinful foods. One needs occasional enjoyment of bad foods for sustained successes (reference balance chapter).

This conversion process took me several weeks to achieve, and every individual is different. The key is association: associating tasty good foods with feeling great about yourself. Once you achieve that feeling consistently you are well on your way to sustained weight loss, and success!

At this point in the book, or process, you have begun your transformation. And quite possibly, some of your bad behaviors have begun to change. At the very least, you have laid the framework for behavioral change. If you have followed the fundamental suggestions I have shared with you, you are exhibiting discipline and change is occurring. You have started to change from the inside out building a foundation of success. Lasting, permanent change must begin on the inside and this is a requirement for lasting change on the outside.

Where is your level of patience, especially with respect to change? Internal change can happen instantaneously, but external, physical change will take some time. Accept this fact now, being patient with yourself. If you are successful being patient with yourself and your progress along the journey, you are almost guaranteed success.

You have now begun change internally; congratulations! It is now time to begin changing externally, to lose weight.

ACTION — Transformation Part 3

It is time to Put Action to Plan

Chapter 10 – New Diet

"Start by doing what's necessary; then do what's possible; and suddenly you are doing the impossible." -- St. Francis of Assisi

It is time to talk about diet. If you are expecting a magical diet or magical diet pill, you will be disappointed. The diet I followed to lose weight and then the diet I have followed to maintain weight loss were each framed with three ingredients: simplicity, taste, and most importantly, self-design. With regard to self design, I learned about nutritional labels, which led to my focus on reducing fat consumption and calories, and I learned about nutritional balance between carbohydrates and proteins. Ultimately, guess what? The key ingredient to weight loss is ingesting fewer calories than what is burned off (through exercise or metabolism). How you go about doing this to lose weight and then, separately to maintain the weight loss (an entirely different program and mindset), the permanent change, is the key.

When I began my weight loss journey in the early 90s, the fitness craze that exists today had not yet taken shape. Weight loss fads existed but they were not in abundance as they are in 2012. The internet had not been invented yet and libraries were full of too much and difficult to locate information. However, Richard Simmons, Weight Watchers and other programs existed in print and on the airwaves. None of that was for me. The existing diet techniques and foods just did not appeal to me. Also, I was just out of college and could not pay for any high-cost solutions. So I created my own. What I would learn was that I did not have to follow any particular program and I did not have to spend any more than I would spend on my old dietary habits.

Early on, I decided to focus on simplicity but I wanted to rid the weight as quickly as I could. As a result, I focused on the fundamentals of reducing calories, eliminating fat, incorporating balance, and introducing foods that I would use to replace the bad foods I was eating. Within this fundamental framework, there are infinite options at your disposal. With all of the options today, these fundamental dieting criteria are the keys for weight loss that worked for me. When I changed my diet, I knew I could fail if I tried to follow some program that did not suit my dieting wants and tastes.

Changing my food choices to healthy foods, including snacks, was absolutely key in my weight loss execution; this continues to ring true today. Finding healthy food choices that are desirable to you is critical to both weight loss and long term success.

<u>Many Choices</u>

Today, diets and diet options are available everywhere you look. The key is to identify healthy tasty foods and snacks and design your own diet; you need to educate yourself such that you must find the tasty, healthy options and replace the nutritionally bad foods with good. Your dietary creation has to be 'yours' to become effective and sustainable. There has never been a better time than now to lose your weight and sustain a healthy lifestyle. And, with diet choices continuing to sprout, and experts continuing to gain more insight on human weight gain and weight loss metrics and tendencies, it should become even easier over time to find good, tasty foods and sustain weight loss.

What Can be Maintained?

The keys to your new diet, in this order, are taste, inexpensive, dynamic and ease. And, eating healthy most of the time. In a latter chapter, I will discuss the "Behavior of Balance". Without ruining the focus of that chapter, one important trick to dieting is never, ever try to be perfect or expect perfection. You will never reach perfection and, if one tries, one will fail. Failure can lead to frustration, and before you know it the likelihood of quitting the diet increases dramatically.

Compounding Interest

Eating healthily, consistently, is like money growing with compound interest. The more healthy foods you consume, the more susceptible to a healthy lifestyle, exponentially, you become. Add exercise to that, which will be discussed later, and then you have even more greatly compounded interest, if that is possible. Or, perhaps a greater rate of compound interest. In either regard, eating healthily one meal after the other creates an incredible fat burning furnace inside you, enabling the potential to lose weight, sometimes a lot of weight. Equally, and conversely, one can go on the opposite direction; eating very poorly with a sedentary lifestyle. This leads to obesity.

Taste

The most important criteria of any diet, if asked to name one, is taste. God has given us food to enjoy. We are not machines that should only intake foods that are not interesting or tasty to us in order to lose weight. No! If the dietary foods you choose to eat are not tasty to you, the likelihood of your diet failing is understandably high. So, you must identify healthy foods that are enjoyable to you.

I have always been a sweets junky; I was before my diet, during my diet and I still am today. When I began losing weight I knew I had to have sweets in my diet; so I incorporated them. I did some taste testing and found the following very tasty to me: Corn flakes, Heath Valley cookies, Archway fat free cookies, fat free ice creams and fat free Fig Newtons. I littered my diet with these foods. I never got sick of them either; in fact, today, I still crave and eat them. In choosing these healthier low/fat free options, and developing an affinity for them, I have been able to withstand the higher calorie and high fat sweets. This still works for me today and I suspect it always will. Note that many fat free foods contain a normal or high amount of calories. So you cannot eat those foods in indefinite quantities. You can still eat those foods but be disciplined about it.

Inexpensive

Cost and the unavailability of choices in the early 90s was a limiting factor of my diet. Today, there are many choices and brands of healthy snacks to choose from, many at low affordable costs. Competition and demand is up, so supply is also up and, as a result, costs are coming down. I am amazed at the choices but I am also a little regretful; I wish that I would have been wise enough to jump on the band wagon of food development, rather than heading into the career I chose: engineering and construction! From coffee shops to grocers, to restaurants, healthy food choices are everywhere.

Dynamic

You must always be on the lookout for new healthy food choices. Restaurants are no exception. Today, one can ask for certain bad foods to be eliminated from prepared restaurant menu choices. This includes butter, full eggs (choose instead egg whites or egg substitutes), replace bad oils with olive oil, etc. The key is to be flexible and always on the lookout.

A popular restaurant in Chicagoland is Portillo's. They have some of the best tasting charbroiled foods I have ever eaten, anywhere. Their hamburgers are untouchable; but they are also very high in cholesterol and saturated fat. I have found a delicious and similarly tasting sandwich at Portillos that I prefer to order over the hamburgers. It is a charbroiled chicken sandwich. I have Portillo's custom make the chicken sandwich for me with ketchup, mustard, and pickle, the same ingredients I use on the hamburger. The resultant sandwich is tasty and low fat. I use this same technique when ordering at most restaurants.

Simplicity

A diet must be simple to execute, extremely tasty, and easy to sustain. If you develop a diet that is too complex, it may become difficult to sustain. An example of this is developing a diet that creates a lot of preparatory work for you when you really do not have the time, such as lunch at work or during the day while you are watching your young children. The diet must be easy; easy to prepare, easy to consistently create and very tasty.

As noted in the Goals chapter, beginning your diet is also beginning a new education on your body, diet, and exercise. One needs to continue to learn about foods to supplement your diet and sustain weight loss. I have to admit that I am always looking into new foods and learning about my body, even nearly 20 years since I lost over 100 lbs.

Diet Example

There are different philosophies and theories about what to eat and when to eat to achieve sustained weight loss and maximized energy levels. Following is an example diet which happens to be the one I followed to lose weight.

Breakfast

- Corn Flakes and coffee for breakfast.

Lunch

- Baked chicken sandwich for lunch.
- Canned green beans.

Dinner

- Baked chicken and rice (with some type of barbeque sauce, along with peppers and pineapple).

Snacks

- Fat free Newtons, cookies, and Corn Flakes throughout the day.

Note

- No food (snacks included) after 6pm.

I followed this diet strictly for 3 months, during which time, along with exercise (next chapters), allowed me to drop 100 lbs. I always felt full, but full of good healthy and tasty stuff. It was incredible; I could eat healthy foods, and enjoy them, and feel full. During the weight loss process, the key was finding healthy foods that tasted good to me and just eat them over and over again. There was no variety with my early weight loss diet but the foods I ate were delicious. It was a drastic, dramatic change for me but the change was pivotal in my weight loss. Today, I am on a maintenance diet, but I easily go back to that diet because it was very tasty and I always felt full. Do I miss Arby's, Dairy Queen, etc.? Emphatically, yes! But my desire, the decision to lose weight, and commitment to change outweighed my desires to consume the bad foods. Today, 20 years later, nothing has changed. I indulge on the bad foods occasionally that I used to eat regularly; I need to do that. However, the decision I made 20 years ago to change is still enforced today.

As mentioned previously, you must take control of your diet when you eat out. Some diets call for a halt to eating out. That is nonsense. Most restaurants offer choices today that are very healthy and filling. When reviewing a menu or ordering a meal, one must focus on fundamental healthy options.

Experiment

During those early years, while not eating out, I experimented with foods at home. At the onset of my weight loss, I created omelets for breakfast on many an occasion. I experimented with fewer egg yolks, straight egg whites, or egg substitute, olive oil instead of butter or lard, chicken and turkey instead of bacon, ham or sausage, and low fat or fat free cheese. I found that the key tastes I enjoy with omelets are the eggs, salt, vegetables, and meats. I also enjoyed the butter flavor somewhat as well.

I learned in the early weight loss years that I could create the tastes I most enjoyed in omelets without the bad, heavy fat ingredients. I was amazed. I found this was the case with most foods I enjoy. I took those learnings out to eat and viola! You can chose healthier, tasty options at restaurants too!

My wife enjoys lower fat foods as well and makes many fantastic low fat dishes, including homemade pizza. Instead of oil/butter, heavy meats and cheeses she replaces them with olive oil, chicken or turkey sausage, and low fat cheeses. Delicious. I have learned that most all of the foods I enjoy can be enjoyed with lower fat, and healthy ingredients.

Tale of Two Omelets

It is not rocket science understanding that every time we eat out, it is our will, hunger and tastes that drive our ordering decisions. Today, we have a great deal of decision-making power when ordering at restaurants. Take, for example, the story of two ladies who arrive at a restaurant around the same time to eat breakfast. One of the ladies was in extraordinary shape and the other was obese. One of the ladies ordered the following omelet: Denver omelet with everything. The other lady also ordered a Denver omelet but with an egg substitute, olive oil in place of butter, and no cheese. After a period, the waiter delivered the omelets to the respective ladies. Unfortunately, the waiter delivered the wrong omelets to the wrong ladies! The seemingly fit lady took a bite and realized it was not what she ordered. The obese lady took her first bit and smiled mischievously. What could have gone wrong? One lady frowned and the other smiled. Something was up – it did not make sense! Well, the fit lady was ready to enjoy a once-in-awhile treat: an omelet full of her favorite, sinful things. On the other hand, the obese lady had ordered the less fat-laden omelet, as she had recently began her diet. She had worked up her will to order the lower calorie fare, which was a big accomplishment early in her journey, but she received the sinful omelet, which caused her defenses to drop. The obese lady smiled mischievously thinking that next time she would eat the healthy omelet but now she would enjoy the unhealthy one!

I made the story up but there are morals. Firstly, most restaurants offer many healthy choices and substitutes across appetizers, main entries, and deserts, and across most meals you choose. So always assertively ask if certain items can be left out or exchanged for healthier ones. Secondly, if you have been on the weight loss journey a while, it is OK to give yourself a break and chose heavier foods. I do this about once per week today. Finally, do not get discouraged during any part of your journey, but most importantly, do not get discouraged at the onset of the journey. A positive mental attitude is critical to success at anything; this is especially true during your weight loss journey.

One must feel free to enjoy going to restaurants, even at the beginning of the journey. For me, I learned that the hard way. For the most part, I stopped eating out entirely for the first two years. I am not a fan at all of salads and I did not think I could find anything appealing at a restaurant that was also low fat. As the old cliché goes, "if I knew then what I knew now" I would have continued eating out at restaurants during the early days of my journey.

<u>Working for You</u>

Make eating work in your favor. Be it to lose weight, gain muscle, reduce cholesterol, ignite cancer fighters, improve blood flow, etc. food is fuel and one of the absolute factors in living healthily.

The foods and quantities you consume and your diet in general will be based on your tastes, reactions to weight loss successes or failures, etc. Over time, you will learn what your body reacts to. Is it a high protein diet, low carb, balanced diet, high caloric intake in the AM, less in the PM, nothing after 6pm, etc., you will need to experiment and your body will let you know what is right. What kind of diet helps you achieve and maintain proper energy levels when you need it most? Learn about different diets, experiment over time and learn what you react to successfully. Most importantly, enjoy the taste!

Diet - Summary and Reflection

- Basic diets that do not require a great deal of thought are the best diets.
- Hold taste high on your dietary requirements list.
- Choose foods that go to work for you. Not all foods; just foods.
- Develop good eating behaviors.
- Develop a list of healthy foods options that you will incorporate across all meals, including snacks.

Using methods, techniques, and like food choices, reviewed in this chapter, build your diet plan.

Chapter 11 – Exercise Plan

Dieting and exercising, together, are required to lose weight. One without the other can ruin the other; or, can cancel out the benefit of the other. Picture a child who is clean, with fresh clothes and newly bathed. If dieting was equivalent to bathing and exercise was the process of washing the clothes, to consistently stay clean, the child would need to diet (bathe) and exercise (wash). If the child would only bathe and continue to wear the same dirty clothes, the child would not be clean. If the child would not bath but continually wear newly washed clothes, the child would still not be clean. Diet and exercise; they go hand in hand like bathing and clean clothes, and they are both equally required for weight loss and a stainable healthy lifestyle. After 20 years, I know this is true. If I have a good week with consistent workouts but I eat poorly (I have done this on vacation), my workouts feel, and probably are, fruitless; I am essentially crossing out my workouts with poor diet. When I diet and workout well, equally, I feel fantastic. This is how I operate, most of the time.

The physical part of healthy living, working out, should only consume about 6% (or about 45 minutes to 1 hour) of your awakened hours during the day, and only

5-6 days per week. Can you invest 6% of your day, 5-6 days a week on your health?

<u>Cardio Workout</u>

Although I played football in high school and college, I was never in good cardiovascular shape. I was big and out of shape. Walking to class in college, typically a 10-15 minute walk, was a burdensome task. I would sweat during the walk, regardless of season and outside temperature, and if stairs were part of my journey, I would often have to stop at the stop of the stair climb to catch my breath. Embarrassed, I would often stop at the top of the stairs, look around, and lean on my knees or the wall, to catch my breath. It was awful; the joys of weighing 300 lbs!

During those days, I would run (I should be honest; slow jog) a mile for cardiovascular training but that is it. I hated running and I never swam or worked out on a stair machine. That had to change if I was to lose weight. This part of my weight loss program was going to be the most difficult for me; and it was.

The eating part was simple; I felt like I was cheating because all of the healthy food I was eating tasted so good to me; I purposely chose tasty, healthy foods. A new cardiovascular exercise regimen, on the other hand, greatly concerned me. My first workout was at a local gym. I hopped on a stair machine and set it to an intermediate level workout. After 5 or so minutes, I had to get off the machine. It was awful and I felt like stopping there. I did not think I could do it but had to keep going. The courage to overcome the first day of my new exercise program was pivotal in my latter weight loss success. Take note of that.

Weight Loss Program

I am not going to sell you on the right program for you but I will share with you the fundamentals of what worked for me. In order to lose weight quickly, and burn fat efficiently, I reached back into my experience with pushups, where I simplified my approach, and applied the same basic ideals. So, rather than begin running, which I hated, my first workout consisted of 3 sets of 5 minutes at the intermediate level on a stair machine. Honestly, I was a bit discouraged with the first day, not feeling entirely confident that I could sustain a life with consistent cardiovascular workouts. I was also nervous about what I had gotten into. Was I capable of losing weight? The next day, I did the same thing, but went in the morning and back to the gym in the evening (doubling my workout). I increased the time I spent on the machine each day, and by the end of the first week, I was doing 3 sets of 15 minutes twice daily. By about the third week, I was up to one set of 40 minutes in the morning and one set of 40 minutes at night. Very good progress. I continued this regimen, 7 days per week, for 3 months. With my new diet plus the information and exercise regimen, I melted 10 lbs a week for 8 straight weeks. This was the basic discipline I discussed in Chapter 7. Begin slowly but maintain a process. Record your progress and see what happens; experience the results.

In hindsight, one of the important things I did my first day, and week, on the new diet and exercise program was stick tightly to my diet and exercise program. Specifically, I did not waiver on lower caloric, low fat foods and I made it to the gym twice daily. Losing that first 10 lbs in week one provided me with confidence and momentum heading into the next seven weeks. So, the important lesson is "stick to the plan". I was not running a marathon, or completing incredible endurance workouts,

I was following a simple process, one that I was always in control of. Also, as or more important, consult your doctor on the exercise and fitness program that you choose.

<u>Plan to Overshoot</u>

I initially lost 125 lbs, hitting a low weight of a around 190 lbs. I could not believe I only weighed 190; it was my plateau. I was continuing my weight loss program at full intensity but I was no longer losing weight. Also, I looked sick and felt too thin, and sensed I was a little underweight. After spending my entire life being big, I also felt a little intimidation of being too small! I decided that I would ease up on my workout but maintain my dietary program. I was charting new territory so I was a little nervous easing up on my diet. So I proceeded to change my workout routine, adding in flexibility and frankly a lot of common sense. Inadvertently overshooting the weight loss mark, in hindsight, was likely one of the best things that could have happened. Specifically, overshooting the mark, allowing some relief in the program while also giving myself what felt like control of my natural weight, was a huge confidence booster. It allowed me to ease my program and comfortably locate the weight that felt most naturally to me. I later settled on a range of weight between 205-212lbs. That was in 1993; and I have been there since.

The effort to lose 125 lbs, and then the decision afterwards to ease into a less aggressive routine, enabled me to establish five very important staples of success.

- Set very high expectations.
- Plan to overshoot your long term weight goal.
- Control.
- Incorporate basic discipline techniques.
- Okay to relax sometimes.

Overshooting my final weight loss "weight", enabled control, gave me confidence, and created a more relaxed approach, which led to a philosophical change in how I view long term weight loss success. This change evolved into a "behavior of balance". I will discuss the behavior of balance in greater detail later in the book. In addition, I am not sure how long I could have continued the aggressive weight loss regimen; it was very tiring. I will provide more insight to this subject below.

Sustained Fitness Program

Those first eight weeks, I had been hitting the gym in the morning and at night, performing the same routine. With the change in direction, I adjusted my plan only slightly. I cancelled my morning workouts and continued my evening workouts, one set of 40 minutes on the stair machine daily.

I also reintroduced weights but only for upper body. My simple routine included bench press twice weekly and arm curls and triceps presses three times per week. I also began to conceive my long term sustained fitness program which was framed by minimal but necessary cardio work (25-30 minutes) and limited weight training. At that point I realized an important lesson that I have affirmed over time. That lesson is this simple: I am not a marathoner, body builder, or triathlete. I am only interested in good health and fitness. Long story short, I did not and do not need a fitness regimen that will cause me to burn out of quickly, both mentally and/or physically. In simpler terms, what I do in the gym must be sustainable for the rest of my life. My life does not revolve around fitness; my fitness supports my life.

Physical and mental burnout is a real possibility if you are spending too much time working out. In 2010,

Chelsea Bush in US News provided "10 Signs You're Exercising Too Much". She goes on to elaborate on the ten ways that your body will tell you slow down before hitting burnout:

1. Decreased performance. A drop in your workout performance is one of the earliest signs of overload, according to Jini Cicero, a conditioning specialist based in Los Angeles, Calif. Altered performance levels are often more apparent in endurance activities such as running, swimming and cycling, she has stated.
2. Disinterest in exercise. A significant decrease in motivation or enjoyment of the activity can be a major sign of burnout, Cicero says. This more often occurs in weight lifters, sprinters or soccer players who are driven by speed and power.
3. Mood changes. Depression, anger, confusion, anxiety and irritability are common when your body is overstressed physically. Those same stress hormones you release when you're emotionally stressed are also released when you're physically overloaded, Cicero explains.
4. Delayed recovery time. Persistent muscle soreness that lasts for hours or days after your workout is a sure sign you need more rest, according to Joseph Ciccone, a physical therapist at Columbia Doctors Eastside Sports Therapy in New York City.
5. Elevated resting heart rate. "When you put more stress on the heart, it has to work a lot harder," Ciccone says. An increase in your normal resting heart rate, say, from 50 beats per minute to 65 beats per minute, could indicate that you're placing excessive stress on your body.
6. Fatigue. Mental or physical grogginess is a hallmark

sign of overtraining, says nutritional biochemist Shawn M. Talbott and author of Natural Solutions for Pain-Free Living, based on his research on overstress patterns in professional athletes. "The knee-jerk reaction to sluggishness is to exercise for an energy boost, but it's a catch-22," he says. "Another workout might wake you up short-term, but you'll be worse off later on."

7. Insomnia. Being in a state of overload often comes with disrupted sleep patterns, so instead of getting that much-needed rest, Talbott says, "you become restless and can't fall asleep."

8. Diminished appetite. "A decrease in appetite can occur in the middle to later stages of overtraining, and goes hand in hand with feelings of fatigue and lack of motivation," says Stenstrup. By slowing down bodily processes like metabolism, the body attempts to force a reduction in its workload.

9. Fat gain. If you've lost weight but noticed an increase in body fat, you could be in the later stages of exercise overload. The body responds to prolonged stress by elevating levels of stress hormones, including cortisol, Stenstrup says. Over time this will lead to increased storage of adipose tissue, as well as inhibit steroid-like hormones that normally help increase muscle. A decrease in muscle mass can cause you to shed a few pounds, but this isn't a good thing since it means your body's less efficient at burning fat.

10. Weakened immune system. Don't try to push through that exercise funk, Talbott warns, "or you'll keep sliding down—to a weakened immune system, inflammation, and outright injury." Not a good thing. Prolonged overtraining can take weeks, even months, to recover from, and can put your health at risk.

I am sometimes amazed at how some people, trainers, and fitness experts approach fitness; like they are training for the Olympics, boot camp, or a Himalayan adventure. Bodies are not made to last, and they will expire more quickly if you work them hard enough. Conversely, fitness regimens need to be designed for minimized joint, ligament, and tendon deterioration and maximized cardiovascular support. That said, if you aspire to achieve incredible human feats in your 40s, 50s, or 60s, more power to you. But just remember, it comes with a price. At some point, you have to stop trying to impress people. After my third year as a collegiate football player, I begin to develop pain in my joints. I was also diagnosed with acute tendonitis in my shoulders. The pain became chronic and I was concerned I would always have it. Fortunately, most of the tendon and joint pain subsided in my 20s, after I had lost weight.

When I first began my diet and exercise program, my journey was much like traveling in a jet; but only comparable to take off and flying at altitude. The take off was like the first phase of weight loss; the engines were maxed out, while I was maximizing my diet and exercise. Then, once altitude or maximum weight loss was realized, I eased off the throttle and began coasting in flight, maintaining an acceptable diet and exercise regimen. I have been flying at altitude for 20 years. Understanding these two phases of the journey is key in weight loss, and sustained weight loss and health.

Some keys I have learned in exercise over the last three decades:

Prepare for:

- Sustained activity over 25 minutes. Determine if you need to remove your mind form the actual physical workout – TV, radio, etc.

Behaviors of Change

- Prepare to think about things you may not normally think about (blood flow sharpens focus).
- Prep to feel great after the workout.
- What type of program can you do the rest of your life? Does that program satisfy the basics of beneficial cardiovascular exercise?
- Understand the basics about cardiovascular health. Master your understanding and the fundamentals.
- Spend enough time working out but do not spend too much time. You will either burn out, you will give up, or your body will give in. The key is balance.
- Do not over complicate your program and plan. Stay focused to the fundamentals.
- When I over do it (and over doing it for me means I don't take a day off soon enough), my body lets me know by giving me a sinus infection. So I am focused on staying the course and getting rest equally.

The exercise program used for weight loss should not be the program used for sustained weight loss. A weight loss exercise program should be geared to efficiently and effectively remove weight. The differences and importance between the weight loss program and the weight maintenance program is discussed in a later chapter. The simple, and well-known, concept or formula to lose weight is reduced caloric consumption, less food, and increased caloric burn through cardiovascular exercise. A sustained weight loss, or lifetime fitness maintenance program, is as simple: a moderately healthy diet and an easy-to-maintain, low impact cardiovascular program.

Become a person who reflects on everything. Develop

a reflection routine. When you begin reflecting on your life deeply, you will recognize opportunities. These opportunities may address deficiencies or improve strengths. You may also question whether or not a perceived opportunity is truly an "opportunity" by seeking a candid opinion from a trusted source: friend, family member, peer or mentor. As discussed previously, it starts with humility; if you build your life around it, the skies the limit for you.

<u>Exercise Plan - Summary and Reflection</u>
Develop an exercise program that works for you. Describe what that will look like.

- Consistency is the key.
- Consult your doctor before beginning your weight loss program.
- Weight loss workouts require much more effort than the subsequent maintenance post weight loss workout.
- There are two phases to weight loss: The act of losing weight and the act of sustaining weight loss.
- Develop a new behavior focused on investing 6% of your day, 5-6 days per week, exercising.
- Describe a week in your life that includes 5-6 days of exercise, comprising 6% of your time each of those days. At what set time will you exercise, or will it be a different time and place each day?

Chapter 12 – So, What Happened?

<u>Physically Speaking</u>
What happens during weight loss? Lets take a look at my journey.

Before I lost over 100 lbs, during the weight loss process, and since I lost the weight? It comes down to the calories; consumption and burn. But there is more to it. The Mayo Clinic notes "Unfortunately, weight gain is most commonly the result of eating more calories than you burn. To lose weight, then, you need to create an energy deficit by eating fewer calories, increasing the number of calories you burn through physical activity, or both."

Let's next take a look at calories, beginning with the "basal metabolic rate" (BMR). The Mayo Clinic describes BMR as "the number of calories your body needs for all its "hidden" functions, such as breathing, circulating blood, adjusting hormone levels, and growing and repairing cells". In short, this is referred to as metabolism. According to Mayo, there are other criteria that affect your metabolic rate, including:

- Body size and composition. The bodies of people who are larger or have more muscle burn more calories, even at rest.

- Sex. Men usually have less body fat and more muscle than do women of the same age and weight, burning more calories.
- Age. As you get older, the amount of muscle tends to decrease and fat accounts for more of your weight, slowing down calorie burning.

Mayo maintains that "your BMR accounts for about 60 to 75 percent of the calories you burn every day." They also assert that, in addition to BMR, two other factors determine how many calories your body burns each day:

- Food processing (thermogenesis). Digesting, absorbing, transporting and storing the food you consume also takes calories. This accounts for about 10 percent of the calories used each day. For the most part, your body's energy requirement to process food stays relatively steady and isn't easily changed.
- Physical activity. Physical activity and exercise — such as playing tennis, walking to the store, chasing after the dog and any other movement — account for the rest of the calories your body burns up each day. Physical activity is by far the most variable of the factors that determine how many calories you burn each day.

Given the aforementioned variables, the picture of what really happened during and after my weight loss becomes clearer. To illustrate, I have taken a look at my BMR at points in time prior to weight loss, during weight loss, and since weight loss.

Behaviors of Change

<u>Before Weight Loss</u>

As an 8th grader in 1984, I was one of the larger kids in my class at 5 foot 8 inches, 190 lbs. I had not yet began playing organized football, and I led a sedentary lifestyle and was very out of shape with a 36 inch waist. Based on my physical statistics, I had a BMR of 2012.

My diet was bad. Below provides a glimpse of my typical daily caloric binge in not only 1984, but several years prior. Keep in mind that a lot of my caloric consumption occurred when no one was around, including my parents. With my stubbornness back in those days, I am certain that if they knew how much I was eating and tried to stop me, I would have figured out how to sneak the food in. I was clearly a bad food addict. Sound familiar?

Using a website (http://www.calorieking.com) to identify calories found in foods I consumed in 1984 (assuming calorie amounts did not change), the following provides my net calorie change on any given day:

Caloric intake:

Breakfast

- Cereal (2 cups plus one cup 2% milk) = 340 calories

Lunch

- Old school cafeteria style lunch - pizza (300 calories), cookie (110 calories),
- green beans (50 calories), and milk (100) calories = 560 calories

Snack

- 2 baloney/mustard sandwiches - 200 calories each = 400 calories
- Chips = 300 calories (2 servings)
- Cookies = 100 calories (Chips Ahoy)

Dinner

- 2 hamburgers = 900 total calories
- Chips = 300 calories
- Workouts: gym class = 150 calories
- Calories burned playing = 150 calories

Calories burned = 300
Calories consumed = 2,900
BMR - 2,012
Net calories - 588 (gained)

Based on my BMR, daily caloric consumption and burn, my net caloric consumption was 588. It is easy to see why I was packing on the pounds early in life. Specifically, the website: www.bmi-calculator.net/bmr-calculator/harris-benedict-equation/calorie-intake-to-gain-weight.php states "if you want to gain body weight, you need to consume more calories than you burn. One pound of body weight is roughly equivalent to 3500 calories, so eating an extra 500 calories per day will cause you to gain one pound a week." As a result, assuming I had a net caloric consumption of 588 calories 5 days a week, I was gaining weight at a rate of 30 pounds per year, which was fairly accurate. Within the calculation, I also assumed that I may have eaten less and played more, or both. I addition, I was getting taller; I was still growing.

Over the next decade, my appetite increased, dramatically. I cannot believe how much I ate. Luckily I was burning a lot of calories at the same time; that said, was gaining weight, big time. By 1993, I was 6 foot 3 inches and 312 lbs, and my BMR had increased to over 2,800. Following was a typical day of calorie binging and burning.

Breakfast

- Cereal (2 cups of cereal plus one cup 2% milk) = 340 calories

Lunch

- 4 cold meat sandwiches - 200 calories each = 800 calories
- Cereal = 340 calories
- Chips = 300 calories

Dinner

Arby's

- 4 roast beef = 400 calories each = 1400 calories
- 4 beef and cheddars = 440 calories = 1760 calories
- Chicken fingers = 590 calories
- Curly fries = 638 calories
- Diet Sprite = 0 calories

Calories burned on the football practice or game field = 3,940
Calories burned = 3,940

Calories consumed = 6,170
BMR - 2,800
Net calories - -570 (lost)

The Arby's dinner occurred only on occasion, given the financial constraints imposed with being a college student. However, the calorie count is consistent across any given dinner, which included football training table most of the time. The -570 lost was during a typical season day however, during the offseason, the calories burned could be reduced by 2,000 or more (calculating in a normal workout session which included weights and light running); as a result, there would have been a substantial net gain during the off season, maybe 2,000-3,000.

Wow. When not practicing, I was consuming unhealthy foods at a rate equivalent to 4 pounds of new weight each week. As a result, although I was building muscle mass through weight training, I was consuming extreme amounts of bad foods and thereby gaining bad weight; e.g., fat. This result was consistent with my size and body composition in 1993.

As discussed in chapters 11, my new diet started during the summer of 1993 and was a drastic departure from the old food binging-based diet. With the new diet, I replaced the bad foods with good, healthy foods and replaced heavy weight training with an extensive, disciplined cardiovascular program. The dramatic changes resulted in the following.

During Weight Loss

- Max weight loss September 1993
- 6-3 190
- 31 inch waist

- BMR 2039

Breakfast

- Corn flakes = 200 calories
- Milk = 90 calories

Lunch

- Chicken sandwich
- Chicken = 185 calories
- Bread = 50 calories
- Sun chips = 140 calories

Snack

- Health Valley fat free cookies = 270 calories - 3 oatmeal raisins

Dinner

- Chicken and Rice = 400+300 = 700 calories

Total = 1635
<u>BMR Formula</u>
Workout = 80 minutes of Stairmaster
From Livestrong.com

Enter your heart rate, in beats per minute, and other individual information into one of the following equations. They are differentiated by gender and solved using a calculator. For men, ((-55.0969 + (0.6309 x Heart Rate) + (0.1988 x Weight) + (0.2017 x Age))/4.184). For women, ((-20.4022 + (0.4472 x Heart Rate) + (0.1263 x Weight) +

(0.074 x Age))/4.184). The resulting number is your caloric burn rate, in calories per minute, at that heart rate.

Calories burned = 1,650
Calories consumed = 1,925
@ 315 lbs BMR = 2,800
Net calories = -2,500 (lost)
@ 195 lbs BMR = 2,050
Net calories = -1,775

With my old diet in June 1993, and prior, produced a net daily calorie gain of 2,000-3,000 calories while the day I began my diet, and during the weight loss process, my net calorie loss was 2,500 calories. That is net caloric change of roughly 5,000 calories! Physically speaking, that net change, represented by my new diet and exercise program, produced the mass weight loss that I experienced during the summer of 1993.

Today, I maintain a net calorie burn of around zero, using the same math used above. Some days I land above and some days below (sometimes drastically, one way or the other). In either event, I do not waste any time worrying about it. Later, in chapter 18, I will provide a graphical illustration and reasoning why I believe your weight loss strategy should occur in two separate phases: Weight loss (net calorie loss) and maintenance (net calorie change equals 0).

Along with a healthy balanced and proper nutrition, combined with tricks that work for you, are the keys to weight loss maintenance.

During your weight loss program, as noted earlier, you must identify foods that help you get through the process. I focused on non fat sweets to help me. You can also eat foods that help you speed up calorie burn. WebMD identifies the following foods that increase caloric burn rate:

Power Up with Protein
The body burns many more calories digesting protein as it uses for fat or carbohydrates. Although you want to eat a balanced diet, replacing some carbs with lean, protein-rich foods can boost the metabolism at mealtime. Healthy sources of protein include lean beef, turkey, fish, white meat chicken, tofu, nuts, beans, eggs, and low-fat dairy products.

Sinless Snacking
Eating more really can help you lose weight -- eating more often, that is. When you eat large meals with many hours in between, your metabolism slows down between meals. Having a small meal or snack every 3 to 4 hours keeps your metabolism cranking, so you burn more calories over the course of a day. Several studies have also shown that people who snack regularly eat less at meal time.

Fuel Up with Water
The body needs water to process calories. If you are even mildly dehydrated, your metabolism may slow down. In one study, adults who drank eight or more glasses of water a day burned more calories than those who drank four. To stay hydrated, drink a glass of water or other unsweetened beverage before every meal and snack. In addition, try munching on fresh fruits and vegetables, which are full of fluid, rather than pretzels or chips.

Step Up Your Workout
Aerobic exercise may not build big muscles, but it can rev up your metabolism in the hours after a workout. The

key is to push yourself. High-intensity exercise delivers a bigger, longer increase in resting metabolic rate than low- or moderate-intensity workouts. To get the benefits, try a more intense class at the gym or include short bursts of jogging during your regular walk.

Build Muscle

Our bodies constantly burn calories, even when we're doing nothing. This resting metabolic rate is much higher in people with more muscle. Every pound of muscle uses about 6 calories a day just to sustain itself, while each pound of fat burns only 2 calories daily. That small difference can add up over time. In addition, after a bout of resistance training, muscles are activated all over your body, increasing your average daily metabolic rate.

Ultimately, using some of the techniques in this book, you must create your own program. Understanding your BMR, coupled with caloric counts within the foods you eat and calorie burn exercises and techniques, will help you recognize what you will need to do to lose weight. After you decide to lose weight, calorie intake and burn rates will change dramatically. Maintaining a discipline program will increase the likelihood of a successful weight loss program and maintenance thereof.

Spiritually and Mentally

In chapter five, I let it all hang out! My faith. I lived through a difficult time supported firmly by His grace. If you are not a believer, that is a decision you must confront, in your heart. If you are a believer, and need His help, lay your burdens with The Lord and, with His strength, support and guidance, transform.

A critical factor that cannot be ignored to ensure change is lasting is the focus on building a foundation. A foundation of learning, understanding oneself, faith, and fundamental knowledge of what is required to initiate change, to change, and to never return to who you once were.

The most substantial change I went through was learning to love and respect 'me'. And the only thing that I recall being as awesome as learning to love and respect myself was realizing that I was capable of loving and respecting myself. There was a time that I truly hated myself; my obesity, lack of maturity, my teeth, everything. The joy felt and experienced knowing that I had incalculable ability to become who I wanted to become was profound. This is an example of what God shared with me when I pleaded for His mercy. He exposed a glimpse of my potential to me. We have such incredible potential in His plan that we can't comprehend, but if we seek from Him a glimpse, and then we experience it, it can be overwhelming.

I began a study of the Bible in earnest about 2 years after my change, learning slowly at first and then joining studies to increase learning and fellowship. And the learning never ends. My study routine today is just that: a disciplined routine. I study in the mornings today, but like my workout and other routines, the Bible study routine will likely change. And, as with everything that is meaningful to you, the key is consistency.

Here is one of many examples of His grace in my life. I have never had an ego. Prior to loving and respecting myself, I felt so inferior and extremely self conscious and unconfident. Egotism was the furthest thought in my mind. After learning to love "me" through the change, I realized how embarrassing, selfish, and irresponsible egotism is, especially to family and close friends. I did a 180 from self pity to self assurance in my abilities, and respect for His creation. If you really are determined to serve others, you feel undeniable shame toward egotism.

And within the heart lives real power. It is where frustration, hate, jealousy, and eventually, personal, professional, and global wars of varying magnitudes develop. It is also the place where real, deep and lasting love resides. Strength to change permanently into something of greater purpose also resides here, in the heart. Choices raised in our minds make the final decisions democratically, seemingly unbiased, even though our hearts have already provided the right answer. This is where God resides.

The heart is a place where either real deep, unimaginably painful darkness exists or the brightest of lights, unfathomable joy, richness enveloped fully by Christ calls home. And the gift of the latter is and has always been our choice.

Our filters, our minds, sometimes skew the important decisions by unwanted years of so called mental maturation. There is no better example of real happiness or real joy than through the unmarred actions of a child, whose heart has yet to be damaged by the sometimes awful maturation of mind. Christ knows this and our tendencies. In Matthew 11:25, Jesus proclaims "I praise you, Father, Lord of heaven and earth, because you have hidden these things from the wise and learned, and revealed them to little children." Children know love.

The good and ugly things that are wafted or equally spewed out of adult mouths is in direct correlation to their filter maturation. This is proven by children. Either one has matured or one is deficient. Most of us can lay claim to these outbursts.

You will truly know someone's level of real maturation by their level of personal control, or, academically speaking emotional intelligence, and by who they are behind public doors, simply evidenced by the culmination of their words and their actions. Where are you, and how is your self control? Your deeply rooted self control will enable your lasting success to change your life, here and in eternity.

At the end of the day, the greatest change potential resides in your heart. Are you ready to allow your years of hurt, frustration, jealously, and anger to be refocused to loving yourself as God loves you? Are you ready to expose your talents to others and do what you are designed to do on earth: help others? Are you ready to allow a patient God to restructure your heart and your life, introducing meekness (strength under control)? He is at your door.

SUSTAINABILITY — Transformation Part 4

Putting up a defense against returning to your old habits, your old self

Chapter 13 — You Have Lost Weight; Now What?

Once you have lost some weight and have been consistent with your new diet, you have developed momentum. After momentum is created it is critical that it is maintained. Maintaining and building momentum will grow your confidence. The longer you maintain your diet, exercise, and weight loss, the greater your momentum and, you may find, the easier it becomes to maintain momentum. When you lose weight, the fat comes off all over the body; legs, stomach, back, shoulders, arms, neck, and face. When one experiences fat loss in these areas, it is an exhilarating feeling. While you notice it, others will as well. This will add to your momentum.

You have reflected on and explored your dietary and exercise lifestyle tendencies, and have contemplated what your defense mechanisms are going to be when confronted with temptations. You have begun to build a solid foundation that will anchor your successful journey.

And, as you begin losing weight, you will learn a great deal about your tendencies toward discipline and consistency to maintain your diet and exercise programs. You will learn what your limits are at the gym and will learn how your conscience will react in fighting temptations. You will find out how to fight hunger with healthy foods as opposed to bad foods and you will learn about patience. Specifically, you may not be burning fat and weight off as quickly as you would like to; are you patient enough to wait for the fat and weight loss? It is critical to your success and sustained weight loss, if you are not already, that you become patient with your body. All the while this is going on, you will begin building new habits and tendencies, and before long, your good habits will far outweigh the bad.

Measurement

While losing weight, progress can be measured by periodically weighing oneself or measuring changes to your waistline. Additionally, clothes will begin to feel loose; this is the true measure. I recall trying a pair of pants on after losing 100 lbs. It was absolutely amazing. I had deflated down to a 32-34 inch waistline. I pulled the size 40 jeans on I wore the last two years in college and drew a big smile. My waist was not the only thing that changed; the circumference of my legs shrunk dramatically. The feeling was remarkable, indescribable.

The Unexpected

During the summer of 1997, my regular fitness routine was to head to the local YMCA at lunch. One day that summer, while I was working out, a lady at the gym approached me, asking if I would be interested in modeling for an artist who created book covers. I was flabbergasted, humbled, but also a little creeped out. Who was this lady and what were her real intentions? After she answered a few of my questions about the specifics, which included a photo shoot with the some production staff at a local business, and that an artist named Alan Pollack would ultimately use the imagines to fashion paintings for a couple science fiction novels, my mind was put at ease. A few weeks later, I spent about 1 hour at the local business, taking what felt like 1,000 photos while holding swords, capes, and other props, although thoroughly exhausted, I walked out feeling pretty good about the whole experience. In 1998, science fiction author RA Salvatore released two books, Demon Spirit and Demon Awakens, with my likeness on the book covers. How crazy is that?

The events leading to the book covers were the results of several coincidences, but one of them was in my control – health and fitness. The indirect result of being included on book covers was the direct result of my decision to lose weight and keep it off. Sometimes in life, you just cannot predict what your decisions and actions will lead to. God's plan for you will lead you down interesting paths.

Buy New Clothes

Once you have dropped weight, and feel your clothes loosening, it is now the opportune time to rid your closet of the big clothes; perhaps giving them to Goodwill, Salvation Army, or another charitable organization. It is important to change your wardrobe as you are changing to sustain your drive to become a new person and to ensure that you will never return to the old person. Keep a pair of pants, however, to remind yourself of who you used to be.

Tell Your Story

Your friends and family will begin to see an exciting change in you. Be prepared to tell your story, but do so in a humble manner. This will give you confidence, inspiration to continue your weight loss, and you will find yourself feeling exhilarated because you will begin your process to inspire others. Once your friends and family begin spreading the word, watch out. And, because other people will begin to learn of your story, you will be compelled to continue with your journey, building momentum.

<u>Learn to Truly Love Who You Are
(if you do not already)</u>

When you lose weight and see what you are capable of it may have a profound effect on you. After I lost over 100 pounds in 1993, I found myself truly loving who I was for the first time in my life. I was in awe of what I accomplished, had an extra skip in my step, and found myself with an incredible amount of confidence that I had never had before.

<u>Some May Not Recognize You</u>

After you deflate yourself, you may find that some or many people you have known for years, may not recognize you. It is a strange, exhilarating yet a little scary. After losing weight, I attended our 1993 BSU homecoming football game. I walked past several people at the stadium who I had not seen in about six months, who glanced and walked past without saying a word. It was surreal. I stopped a few guys, introduced myself and shook hands. That was fun. One of my old friends asked if I was sick, which caught me off guard.

<u>Work Diligently To Prevent a Relapse</u>

After you have completed the weight loss phase of your journey, you have received a gift, one that you must be careful not to damage or lose. Lean on your source of energy and ensure that you do not relapse.

<u>Help Others with Action and Encouragement</u>

You must seek out people who are struggling with their weight problem and encourage them to change. In doing this, be very perceptive however, of the state at which the other person may be in. They may be over sensitive to their problem and may be embarrassed about a stranger or even someone they know, approaching them about the problem.

Condition Yourself that You are a New Person to Never Return to the Old You

As you lose weight and fat, and are essentially becoming a new person, you must understand that you are becoming a new and improved you. It is important to mediate on the new you and reflect on how badly you used to feel and how great you feel now. This reflection will become positive reinforcement in your journey, helping you combat your natural tendencies to overeat, skip workouts, and return to the old you.

Raise Your Personal Standards and Expectations of Yourself

Reflect, enjoy and be proud of your accomplishments to date. Celebrate those accomplishments.

Aspire to Become a Continuous Learner of Diet and Exercise, as well as New Trends

As I encouraged earlier in this book, you must begin to learn about health and diet if you are unfamiliar with these topics at the onset of your program. And it must not stop. As time has passed, I have been amazed at how different perspectives, diets, foods, and exercise programs have evolved over 20 years. Much of the evolution has been based on experts leaning more on the affects of fitness and health on the human body. This evolution will surely continue. New diet foods and exercise equipment are being developed all the time, and current programs and equipment are getting better. It is critical to stay on top of these changes and become an active and continuous learner. The more you know, the more equipped and knowledgeable you become during your journey; the more apt you will be to have sustained success. Most importantly, you must learn and understand your tendencies, and understand how the foods you consume affect your body.

Understand that You are Becoming a Legitimate Weight Loss Expert

Once you have a lost weight, you are now an expert at weight loss. You know what it takes, what it feels like, the discipline that is required, and as a result you are an expert. Develop confidence in your expertise.

Understand that You Need to Help Others with Similar Challenges You Faced

You have lost weight, changed your life, likely incurred some confidence you have never had. Now you are now obligated to help people lose weight; and it is really easy. Helping others requires two things: listening to someone who needs help and then encouraging them to change.

Develop Your Own Techniques

Prepare to encounter change in overweight people you know. They may become inspired by you, but they may also become angry with you, jealous, hateful, or even embarrassed (at themselves) to be around you. Take this as a challenge in your development to be patient with anyone who shows frustration with you because of your change. Focus on listening, understanding and offering help, if or when it is requested.

Prepare to deal with setbacks and set up a risk mitigation plan. For example, if you relapse and overeat, you need to regroup, study the cheat sheets, look at yourself in the mirror and fight back. Please do not take this as relapsing is an option, or is OK, because it is not. Perfection can never be expected, but keeping the right mindset and focus is expected to achieve sustained weight loss and change.

You Have Lost Weight; Now What? - Summary and Reflection

- You have lost weight. Congratulations! Now, ease off of the physical exertion but exercise steadily and confidently.
- Do not forget humility.
- Help others with your new found gift!

Chapter 14 — Diet and Exercise Constraints

We all have a bag of excuses or interruptions in life that can derail most best laid plans. This is a given, a fact, so it is important to identify the potential interruptions that may prevent your change from occurring. As important as understanding you will have roadblocks and excuses on your way to weight loss and sustained weight loss, you must think about the obvious dietary and exercise constraints that exist in your life and develop plans to mitigate your risks. I have encountered excuses and fight them all the time. You must define clearly what the excuses are, and then plan against and fight the natural tendencies engrained in your psyche that could easily prevent your dreams of changing your life.

<u>Diet</u>
Never be fooled that your work schedule or travel, or both, prohibit good dietary practices. In fact, most locales, at the farthest reaches, offer low fat and caloric alternatives. From 2001 to 2004, I traveled 4 days a week, and, to make matters more difficult, from 2002-2004, I was also earning my MBA. During that time, I could have easily given up my diet, my exercise program, or both, regressing back toward the old me. However, instead,

I learned a lot about fast food, sit down restaurant, and convenience store healthy choice alternatives. Although I developed tricks and techniques of healthy eating on the road, I have to state that I am a convenience store addict. The choices at national drug store and gasoline chains offer amazingly healthy alternatives. In fact, today, if my hunger pains drive to do so, I will stop at a convenience store on my way home to pick up dinner! The only sad part of that story is that I drive 15 miles from work to our doorstep! In all honesty, healthy food choices and alternatives abound. There are no real dietary constraints; only will power failures.

<u>Exercise</u>

When I began losing weight, I worked out both in the morning and at night. I was obsessed but, more importantly, I was excited about becoming a new person. After three months of this regimen, which helped to generate an approximate 120 pound weight loss, I eased up to working out only at night. I continued my nightly workout regimen for the next five years. After starting a new job, it became impossible for me to workout in the morning, and my commute left my evenings short; so I hit the gym at lunch. I worked out at lunch for the next eight years, through another job change, until I changed to mornings in 2009, when we bought a treadmill. I worked out in our basement from 2009 to 2011. After the treadmill broke, I joined a local gym, working out in the morning.

The point is there seems to never be a good or easy time to work out. It is easy to make excuses to skip a work out or to not work out at all. As noted earlier in the Contract chapter, it is critical that you identify the best time to work out and develop a routine around that time.

Be it in the morning, at lunch, or at night, you can find the time. Over time, it is even more critical that you develop the virtue of flexibility.

Incidentally, the first three years after beginning my diet and exercise routine to change my life physically, I used a stair machine. I have since used a treadmill. While using the stair machine, I always leaned on the handrails. A huge misnomer then and now was that one should not use those handrails! I recall, after losing about 50 lbs (after 5 weeks I might add), a nice lady approached me while I was on the stair machine stating something along the lines of, and in an arrogant manner, "that is not how you are supposed to use that equipment". "Baloney", I thought! Look, I lost over 100 lbs using the handrails. Do not be fooled into thinking you should not use the handrails. You can still lose weight, a lot, in fact, by holding on to the handrails. The bottom line is develop your routine and stick with it! The weight will come off and stay off. If or when I switch back to a stair machine, I will use the handrails. Period.

<u>Diet and Exercise Constraints - Summary and Reflection</u>

- Identify your constraints and work to mitigate them.
- Be determine to create time to workout.
- Be flexible.

Chapter 15 – Offer and Acceptance - Your Contract

Sometimes you just do it. But some of us need a framework and accountability to entice us to see things through. Enter a contract. I used a contract for about 12-13 years after I lost weight. This helped me stay on my change course. I reviewed the contract each morning when I awoke, establishing a precedent for the day ahead. It worked.

During the process of weight loss and sustained weight loss, I learned there is power in developing and executing a personal contract, especially if it is tied to the specific goals you have established. A contract can provide you with a subconscious reminder of the importance, credibility and legitimacy of the decision you have made and the goals you have established to fulfill your decision. In short, a contract can solidify your personal commitment to achieve your goals. The contract should be fundamental and specific, should have an expiration date, and should reflect your new goals, and should provide you with a signature block for authorization. A sample contract to support your goals follows:

I, Steve Jones, on June 1, 2013, for the purpose of transforming my life, shall adhere to a structured weight loss program until I have lost 100 lbs. This contract shall be enforced through June 1, 2014.

(Note that your contract should have an established start and end date. You will need to establish a new contract when the old contract expires.)

I shall adhere to the goals I have established, which include:

(Goals copied from chapter 9)

<u>Mental</u>

Assuming your change program is starting in June:

- *Learn basics about nutrition and proper dieting. Select book by July 1 and finish by August 31.*
- *Learn basics about cardiovascular exercise by July 15.*
- *Obtain and listen to a grammar improvement tape collection.*
- *Review your diet and exercise plans with your Dr. for input.*

<u>Physical</u>

- *Establish a regular workout philosophy, and execute. That is, I will run on treadmill, outside, or equivalent cardiovascular exercise, 5 days per week before 6am. If I miss one of my 6 am workouts, I will make up that workout the same day before 1pm.*
- *I will rest no more than 1 day per week and not workout.*

- *Maintain energy by eating low fat or fat free snacks regularly.*
- *Stair machine at least once daily, 7- days per week.*
- *Sauna once daily.*
- *Weight training at low weights and high reps 2 days per week.*

An exercise plan is discussed in detail in chapter 11.

Diet

- *I will establish my regular dietary foods.*
- *I will establish the frequency I will allow myself to cheat.*
- *Remove all fat laden foods from my diet immediately with no cheating whatsoever until I arrive at a weight I felt comfortable at.*
- *Ingest only low fat or fat free foods.*
- *Do not ingest any foods after 6pm.*

Dietary specifics are contained within chapter 10.

Weight Loss

- *25 lbs in first 6 months*
- *50 lbs in first year*

Steve Jones   Date

By authorizing this contact, you accept the conditions that you have established. This is your contract, to be used and seen only by you. The effort and action to write and authorize a contract will fortify your plan to lose weight and stay healthy on your journey.

Offer and Acceptance - Your Contract - Summary and Reflection

- Your plan to change is a contract between you and yourself.
- The contract to self solidifies your intentions and action to lose weight and to keep it off.
- Strengthen your new disciplined behavior by virtue of a personal contract.
- Develop a contract.

Chapter 16 – Behavior of Balance

We have reviewed the importance of your decision to lose weight and change your life, reflection on your life experiences, incorporating personal faith in your decision and the importance of setting a solid foundation for future success. We have also discussed the keys to fundamental discipline, how to develop a new diet and exercise program, and the potential constraints that must be addressed which may limit or prevent you from executing those programs. Building the foundation for success and executing to the plan are critical to your successful weight loss strategy. However, sustained weight loss is a different challenge unto itself.

Perfection is impossible and constant pursuit of perfection can physically and mentally wear anyone out, and will eventually cause you to fail or to become discouraged; potentially failing in such a way that could cause you to permanently end your journey. Perfection is not possible; but what is possible is understanding a pace that is acceptable for weight loss maintenance, a pace that is acceptable to you. Either you achieve success at a pace you design and can operate within the rest of your life, or you become overwhelmed and discouraged that you cannot possibly do what "they do" (hard core fitness enthusiasts, athletes, trainers, fitness professionals, etc), or you do what "they do" for a period of time, or you continue the pace you were under while losing weight, but then burn yourself out. You give up. Here is what I mean:

Pursuits of Excellence can be Overwhelming

Within many athletic pursuits across the world, impressive acts of strength, will power, and endurance are ever present. One can easily find stories about professional and amateur athletes accomplishing incredible feats in the fields of agility, such as gymnastics, or endurance, as in marathoners and triathletes, and strength, as in football, power lifting, etc. People around the world work very hard to achieve the incredible feats of their performances. They deserve much adulation for perfecting their respective crafts. I recall the effort required to be a collegiate athlete, the work involved, discipline required, and sustained efforts on the field and classroom. It was very difficult and I was an average player. It is easy to respect and be in awe of those who achieve great feats.

What also lies in these incredible successes can be a perception of "that is what I need to do to for sustained weight loss". I have to be perfect to achieve the weight loss strategies I aspire to achieve. I have had these thoughts, especially early in my weight loss journey. I would see people in magazines, the internet, on TV, even in the gyms I worked out at. I honestly felt overwhelmed at times at the agility, strength, and endurance that some people displayed. I saw what I felt was perfection in the abilities of others and often felt overwhelmed at my imperfect abilities and imperfection in general, as a result. I became discouraged at times, wondering how could I run that fast or for that length of time, and continue doing that during my journey, the rest of my life. I really got hung up on this 'perceived perfection'. I reflected a lot on these feelings and, luckily, came to the realization that I did not have to be perfect with my diet and exercise program. I learned that perfection is simply a perception and should not be the focus. I believe a lot of people get discouraged with the perception of perfection in others, which derails a lot of diet programs, especially after losing weight. That is unfortunate.

I am not condoning mediocrity at all, but longevity. To achieve the latter, physically and mentally, there has to be a balanced output. Having a sense of balance within the emotional, mental, and physical investment of your health is the only way to achieve success the rest of your life.

Consistency Not Perfection

After you lose weight, do not get hung up on a perfect diet, a perfect exercise program, or the perfect weight. Do not get hung up with perfection! For long term, permanent weight loss, any pursuits of perfection must be avoided at all costs. Your new motto should be 'I strive to maintain consistent imperfection'! Not really, but sort of. Consistency is key. Pursuits of perfection are fine for the short term but the general pursuit of perfection for long term weight loss can become a dangerous obstacle to one's success. For example, if your exercise program includes a cardiovascular regimen of 4 days of running for 25 minutes per day, your focus should be to consistently get to the place you prefer to run (track, treadmill, road) and complete the work. That is it. Perfection, or hard core fitness, should never be one's long term intention or goal, however, knowing what perfection means is very important. If you hold your long term diet or exercise program to standards that are too rigid, you become more susceptible to failure because of the difficulty of sustaining a rigid program over the long haul.

Simplicity

Today, I try to watch what I eat, most of the time (85-90%) and workout 4-5 days straight on cardio equipment (a stair machine, treadmill, or an elliptical machine), then take a day off in between in order to rest. I also perform pushups, curls and triceps exercises twice weekly. That is it. If I wanted to, I could hike, bike, run in races, etc., The key is being persistent, consistent, and, at the end of the day, maintaining the mindset that whatever I do I will continue a 4 days straight, one day off, cardio routine. Nothing more.

Behavior of Balance

The culmination of imperfect forms of diet and exercise leads to the "Behavior of Balance" theory. In short, the Behavior of Balance is all about striving for ranges rather than particulars. This concept involves relaxing on diet and exercise for long term health rather than ensuring that specific goals (weight, exercise frequencies, diet) are being met. The Behavior of Balance concept should be part of weight loss maintenance but should not be part of the initial part of the journey, during weight loss.

I discovered this principle in the late 90s, after meeting my future wife. Before Behavior of Balance, I was very hard on myself, working out 6 or 7 days straight, heavy lifting, the works. I was tired and could always feel fatigue setting in or failure on the horizon, or in the periphery. I was punishing myself at times. Our vacations and overnight trips, or simply every day plans, first involved "where and when will I workout?!" I needed to relax a little but was somewhat fearful of that, of any slight change creating a reversal back to who I was. In hindsight, how ridiculous was that line of thinking? In addition to fatigue, I often battled colds and sinus infections, so many in fact that in 2000 I needed nasal surgery to rid the persistent, backed up infection lying caked in my sinuses. My body was giving up. Luckily for me, my wife taught me to relax and not be so particular about how much I worked out and helped me to get back to enjoying the foods I like. That change was a significant event for me because I was afraid to lose the gift I had received, the weight loss, lifestyle, the change. Over time I realized that, to my surprise, I did not gain the weight back. Today, given me mindset and the techniques shared in this book, I know the weight will not come back.

In hindsight, although I slowed down my diet and exercise regimens after losing over 100 lbs 20 years ago, immediately after the weight loss, I sometimes continued to work out and diet as if I was losing weight. I did not need to diet and work out that way. I should have changed course immediately and begun following the Behavior of Balance theory. Further in this chapter, I provide example practices that adhere to the Behavior of Balance theory that you may consider using after you have lost the weight you planned to lose and you are entering a maintenance phase of change.

The Behavior of Balance requires you to initially understand your weight loss and health needs in diet, weight, and exercise. Once you have an understanding established, and the specific goals are established, those goals are stretched into ranges. For example, if your weight goal is 150, the Behavior of Balance equivalent may be 145-155. Maintaining weight loss using the Behavior of Balance, is all about setting limits and buffers around those goals to allow you to operate without the pressures of specifics. Operating using the Behavior of Balance theory will set your mind at ease and set you free. Examples of how the Behavior of Balance may be applied to diet, exercise and weight follow:

Behavior of Balance – Diet
When eating, do not focus on the perfect diet, ever. Instead, focus on a balanced diet of good healthy foods and, occasionally, bad foods.

Write bad foods into your program! Identify foods and quantities which are of the approximate volume needed to curb your hunger and the approximate health value needed to maintain a healthy lifestyle.

I have always had a sweet tooth, then and today. I still eat a lot of sweets however there is a huge difference in the type of sweets I eat today compared with what I ate 20+ years ago. My sweet tooth 20+ years ago involved all the bad sweets, you name them, beginning with full out bad-for-you ice cream. Today, I still enjoy ice cream but only low/non fat versions. And, when I indulge in ice cream, I do not eat a cup full; I still eat a large bowl full.

Behavior of Balance – Exercise
With exercise, ease up, be flexible and find the appropriate workout program that allows you to sustain the weight level you have achieved. This may be walking, aerobics, jogging, stair machine, a combination of the aforementioned, or something entirely different. The key is simplicity and flexibility, ensuring that you keep your heart rate at an acceptable fitness level.

Behavior of Balance – Weight
If your plan is to weigh 150 lbs, focus on a range of, for example, 145-155. If your weight falls within that range, you have reached your goal, your expectation!

Becoming Routine

At some point, your diet and exercise programs, with the Behavior of Balance incorporated within them, will become routine, becoming who you are. When you understand your body's limits and reactions to foods, and combine that with Behavior of Balance, you will have reached a stage of "no return" in your pursuits of long term health. No return, in this case, means never returning to the person you had decided to change. You will find that, no matter where you are, eating well and exercising will occur. You will understand what your body needs to be fit and when to take breaks in your diet and exercise program.

Not Immediate

Please note that I am not endorsing incorporating the Behavior of Balance theory at the beginning of your weight loss journey. Your weight loss program, the first phase of the journey, needs to be strict and disciplined. Losing weight must be an efficient and effective process. After you have lost the weight, reaching your weight loss goal, now it is time to incorporate the Behavior of Balance. Just like weight loss in an early chapter is analogous to taking off in a commercial airliner, the Behavior of balance, is akin to flying at altitude. The thrust is no longer at full power but at a percentage of full power.

Like your body, if you run at full throttle too long you will stop flying because you will run out of gas, your "parts" will experience fatigue and wear out, or both. Eventually, if you continue to run at full throttle, your parts will wear out. The ultimate goal with sustained weight loss is to identify the appropriate level of fitness and then work to sustain that level. Maintaining this approach, this behavior across all areas of what enabled your change, will create a sense of equilibrium across the three key areas impacted by your physical change (weight, diet, and exercise).

Behavior of Balance – Summary and Reflection

- Be consistent and do not consider perfection.
- Perfection is not possible but reaching the bounds or limits of perfection is possible and sustainable.
- What is the approximate diet and exercise regimen you want to follow? Not specific. Set your expectations on a certain weight and set your diet your diet to approximate foods to eat and calories to consume.
- Learning the "Behavior of Balance". That is, the diet and exercise Behavior of Balance. The concept is simple. What is the approximate foods types and calorie consumption levels you intend to focus to, and the approximate exercise program you intend to conquer. Not specific but approximate.
- And maintaining this range allows you to reach an equilibrium across the three areas (weight, diet, and exercise).
- Develop the criteria of your Behavior of Balance and execute, in a disciplined manner until it becomes reactionary. You will know it is reactionary when, you are confronted with a dietary or exercise challenge, you have options and you execute without hesitation. Until that time, you must follow the program you have developed.
- Establish the behaviors to address your deficiencies and ensure you stick to them. Don't measure your

Behaviors of Change

diet meal to meal, but week to week. If you stay within the Behavior of balance over time, the weight will be kept off. If you focus on a meal, or skipped workout, you will drive yourself nuts. Focus on the behavior over time. Picture the behavior as a graph. If you plot your diet and exercise, what are the averages for both over time? Are you within the behavior?

- It's important that this is understood with respect to your body. This is not something you should follow with a checklist or monitor every minute. Conversely, this is something you should develop an understanding of in your head only. It takes time and practice.
- Identify your behaviors of balance. Develop an outline of how the Behavior of Balance can be incorporated into your plan.
- The Behavior of Balance is the key to sustained weight loss. However, do not incorporate the Behavior of Balance concept until the desired weight has been removed.

Chapter 17 — Pulling Everything Together for the Long Haul

We have reviewed a behavioral change journey, a change process involving reflection, spirituality, discipline, execution, and sustainability. The following captures the process graphically, providing a big picture perspective.

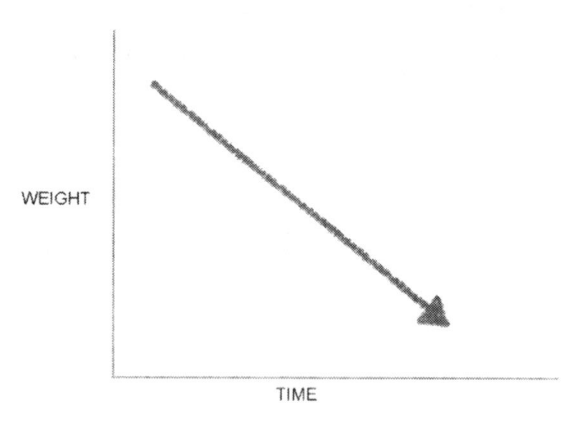

BAD PLAN - BURNOUT
Physical burnout
Mental burnout
Over commitment
Failure

This plan is too hard, too fast, unrelenting, never resting, over-committed, burnout, and leads to failure

Behaviors of Change

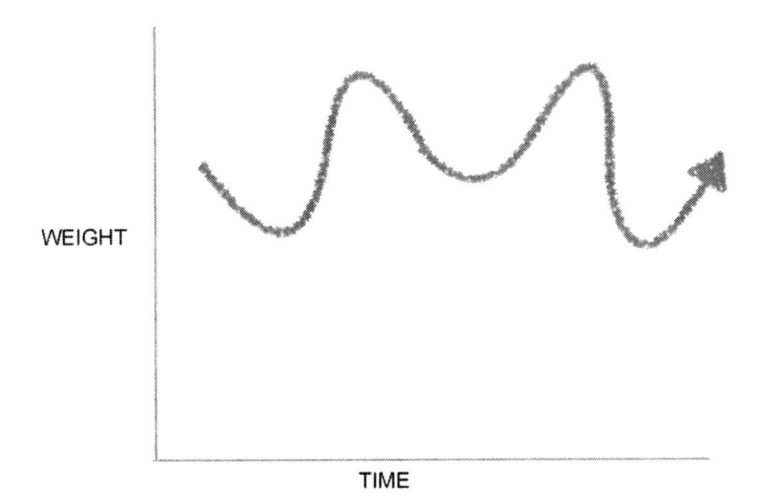

BAD PLAN - YO YO DIET
No commitment
No emotional tie to success
Unsustainable plan
Failure

This plan depicts yoyo dieting and exercising, is non-committal, inconsistent, and leads to failure

[Graph: WEIGHT vs TIME with a slightly upward-sloping arrow]

BAD PLAN - NO PLAN
No interest in change
Laziness
No action
Failure

This plan depicts intimidation and laziness; there is no change, no action, and no commitment, leading to failure

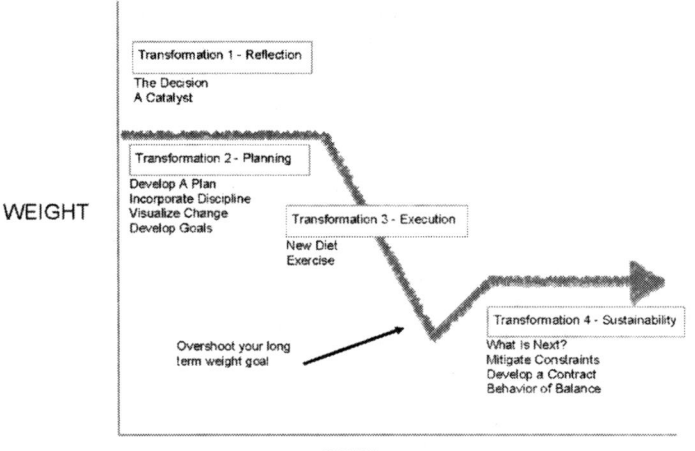

Behaviors of Change

```
                Transformation 1 - Reflection
                The Decision
                A Catalyst

                    Transformation 2 - Planning
                    Develop A Plan
                    Incorporate Discipline
WEIGHT              Visualize Change      Transformation 3 - Execution
                    Develop Goals
                                          New Diet
                                          Exercise

                                                              Transformation 4 - Sustainability
                          Overshoot your long                 What Is Next?
                          term weight goal                    Mitigate Constraints
                                                              Develop a Contract
                                                              Behavior of Balance

                                          TIME
```

SOLID PLAN FOR LASTING CHANGE

This plan is balanced, achievable, is more controlled, and leads to lasting weight loss and success.

With diet and exercise, never try to reach perfection consistently but know how perfection feels. Since I lost over 100 lbs nearly 20 years ago, one thing I have learned is that maintaining a perfect diet and perfect exercise regime is impossible. Why is it impossible? For us normal folks, sustained perfection wears us out; introduces mental and physical fatigue and muscle, tendon and ligament strain. If your goal is to lose weight, and sustain your weight loss for the rest of your life, you first have to realize that minimums are more important than maximums. Maximums include things like never eating the things you want to eat or running marathons or triathlons the rest of your life. I am not saying either is bad but if you believe that people serious about sustained health, diet and exercise must be personal trainers, athletes, etc. you are wrong.

While I was growing up, I was not educated in healthy living, I had a poor diet, I did not exercise to be fit, and I lacked health discipline. I fit the mold of most people. These are the specific reasons why I was overweight.

Sustained diet and exercise first begins with reflecting and understanding where you are and where you want to go. What you should eat and how you should exercise, to maintain good health. Then, putting a plan together and executing to the plan. That is it. A sustained diet and exercise plan should not include training for 5Ks, marathons, or triathlons; unless that is your prerogative. What I have learned over the years is that you must find your minimally good diet and exercise regimens and maximum regimens. This as well as being flexible is what I refer to as the Behavior of Balance.

Little Behavioral Change Anecdotes

- Simplicity.
- Doing enough but not overdoing.
- Prepare yourself to become disciplined for the rest of your life.
- Be patient with yourself.
- By developing discipline and acting on your words, you will change your life, and very likely, lives around you.
- DO not look down at those who are not disciplined, who are struggling with their health but rise up and help them! Share your learnings with them, encourage them, and help them to turn around their circumstances and begin losing weight.
- There is always time.
- Staying focused and staying on schedule!
- Develop techniques and tricks.

- Fighting late night hunger.
- Develop tricks for travel.
- Snacking throughout the day on healthy and pseudo healthy items minimizes hunger and binging.
- When you are starving, stop eating before you fill yourself too much.

After you have reflected on your life and disposition, you have lost weight, now develop your own timeline and keep it near you; develop your story. Be creative. Talk to your friends, family, and acquaintances about it without being boastful. Indirectly, you are asking them to hold you accountable to sustained weight loss because the next time you see them you have stayed disciplined, focused, and successful! You can inspire them.

In 5, 10, 50 years, encourage someone that needs to lose weight or has lost a lot of weight – that they can do it too. Be a champion of sustained weight loss, sustained success!

Early on, look for failure warning signs. Be mindful and careful of doing too much, becoming intimidated by diet and workout routines, or becoming intimidated by those people who appear to be super human in the gym. They are as vulnerable as you are, and are more greatly prone to burnout sooner rather than later. Remember, it's a short term sprint to lose weight and change, and then a less intensive journey to maintain weight loss, becoming a different person. Continual sprinting will lead to burnout and failure.

Chapter 18 — Behaviors of Change - Your Journey

So, lasting change requires behavioral change across all facets of life. Assessing all facets of life and developing an action plan to change across all areas is required for permanent, sustained change. It all starts with behaviors and a willingness to reflect on your life, openly and constructively. Behavioral change is a gift.

We began with my journey and my experiences; have you started your journey to change? Where are you in your journey? Are you frustrated or hurting, are you in decision now about your impending change, have decided to change, have visualized and are now planning your new life, or have you began your transformation? Or have you experienced a full inside and outside transformation? If the latter actions are true, you have unveiled a gift that you have always had. If not true, unveil that gift! If you believe you have not received your gift, it's time to acknowledge receipt because it is there, by virtue of God. Accept the gift now and begin your journey of change. You can do it! And, when you achieve change, do not be surprised when people who need change to envelop their lives reach out to you for help. With a humble heart, help them.

Behaviors of Change

A foundation of behavioral change must be laid before lasting change can occur. A foundation comprising attitude, intelligence, action, evidence, sharing, and helping others will ensue. But first, it all begins with you.

You will do it!

- Reflect on you.
- Identify your fuel.
- Learn basics about weight loss and metabolism.
- Know where your starting point is.
- Understand basic discipline, apply it to your life.
- Be humble.
- Work yourself to an acceptable level of weight loss. Then, after losing, work yourself into an acceptable level of weight and health maintenance. Nothing more, nothing less.
- Help others.
- It is time to change, inside then out!

References

Chapter 1
"Summary Health Statistics for U.S. Adults: National Health Interview Survey", 2005. Accessed December 3, 2012, http://www.cdc.gov/nchs/data/series/sr_10/sr10_232.pdf

Chapter 2
"Scout Camp, Player Evaluation Results", the Austin Group, March 21, 1993, a professional football preparatory event in Chicago.

Chapter 3
"The Effect of Fast Food Restaurants on Obesity and Weight Gain" by Janet Currie, Stefano DellaVigna, Enrico Moretti, Vikram Pathania. NBER Working Paper No. 14721. Issued in February 2009. Accessed January 26, 2013,
http://www.nber.org/papers/w14721

"Census of Retail" Accessed January 26, 2013,
http://graphics8.nytimes.com/images/blogs/freakonomics/pdf/Seth1.pdf

THE SUPER SIZE OF AMERICA: AN ECONOMIC ESTIMATION OF BODY MASS INDEX AND OBESITY IN ADULTS by Inas Rashad, Michael Grossman, Shin-Yi Chou
Working Paper 11584, August 2005. Retrieved January 26, 2013 from http://www.nber.org/papers/w11584

"Health, United States", 2008. Accessed January 26, 2013, http://www.cdc.gov/nchs/data/hus/hus08.pdf

"The 'Unhealthy' Food Network", Kimberly Snyder, C.N., January 23, 2012. Accessed January 23, 2012, http://kimberlysnyder.net/blog/2012/01/23/is-the-food-network-supporting-obesity/

"The Merck Manual Home Handbook". Accessed July 1, 2012, http://www.merckmanuals.com/home/disorders_of_nutrition/obesity_and_the_metabolic_syndrome/obesity.html

"Eating Disorders, The American Psychological Association". Accessed July 1, 2012, http://www.apa.org/helpcenter/eating.aspx

"Obesity and severe obesity forecasts through 2030". Finkelstein EA, Khavjou OA, Thompson H, Trogdon JG, Pan L, Sherry B, Dietz W. Source Health Services and Systems Research Program, Duke-NUS Graduate Medical School, Singapore. Accessed July 15, 2012, http://www.ncbi.nlm.nih.gov/pubmed/22608371

Chapter 5
"Pro Football Weekly" Vol. 7, No. 28, May 1993. 1993 Draft Preview

"Our Lads Guide to the NFL Draft", April 1993

Chapter 6
"There are risks and costs to a plan of action. But they are far less than the long-range risks and costs of comfortable inaction" John F. Kennedy, 35th President of the United States of America. Accessed August 1, 2012, http://www.quotationspage.com/quote/29333.html

Chapter 7
"When Everyone Gets a Trophy, No One Wins" Michael Signman April 18, 2012. Accessed July 1, 2012, http://www.huffingtonpost.com/michael-sigman/when-everyone-gets-a-trop_b_1431319.html

"Albert Puhols", Michael O'Horo, Blog. Accessed January 26, 2013, http://blog.rainmakervt.com/post/7817463307/what-does-albert-pujols-do-that-you-dont

"Play Hard, Practice Harder", Melissa Issacson, ESPN on September 10, 2009. Accessed January 26, 2013, http://sports.espn.go.com/chicago/columns/story?columnist=isaacson_melissa&id=4463664

"Habits" by Darren Hardy, June 3, 2010. Accessed January 26, 2013, http://mysuccessfilledlife.com/2010/06/03/habits-by-darren-hardy/

"Walter Payton's off-season training" by Joseph Staph, November 1, 2006. Accessed October 1, 2012, http://magazine.stack.com/TheIssue/Article/3888/Walter_Paytons_offseason_training_.aspx

Chapter 11
"Start by doing what's necessary; then do what's possible; and suddenly you are doing the impossible." By St. Francis

of Assisi. Accessed January 26, 2013, http://thinkexist.com/quotation/start_by_doing_what-s_necessary-then_do_what-s/219816.html

Chapter 12
"10 Signs You're Exercising Too Much", by Chelsea Bush, November 5, 2010. Accessed November 1, 2012, http://health.usnews.com/health-news/blogs/on-fitness/2010/11/05/10-signs-youre-exercising-too-much

Chapter 13
"Metabolism and weight loss: How you burn calories", The Mayo Clinic Staff. Accessed October 12, 2012, http://www.mayoclinic.com/health/metabolism/WT00006/

"BMI Calculator, Calorie Intake to Gain Weight". Accessed July 1, 2012,
www.bmi-calculator.net/bmr-calculator/harris-benedict-equation/calorie-intake-to-gain-weight.php states

Chapter 14
"The Demon Spirit", by R. A. Salvatore, January 30, 1999.

"The Demon Awakens", by R.A. Salvatore, February 28, 1998.